"This beautiful book is a testament and inspiration to those who may feel that soulmate love has passed them by. The authors demonstrate that love found later in life can have a depth and maturity that is uncommon in younger years. This kind of love takes skill, patience, and a deep inner knowing that is attained through life experience. If you have given up on finding love later in life or feel uninspired in your current relationship, I highly recommend this book. It just may show you that the best is yet to come."
~ Nancy Harris
Holistic therapist, and transformational life coach

"A sacred soul story of trust and faith on the journey to finding love later in life! I've known Pat for over a decade and witnessed her deep desire and personal journey to find aligned love. Her journey to attracting Larry into her life will open your heart and remind you that love is always within reach when you keep your heart open."
~ Linda Joy
Bestselling Publisher & Publisher of Aspire Magazine

"Finally, a book that updates the modern-day love story. Pat and Larry prove that manifesting a relationship like theirs takes mutual deep work and the ability to let God lead. I don't know what's more heartwarming; the fact that they found each other later in life or the fact that their love story is true."
~ Donna Rustigian Mac
Executive Communication Coach/Workforce Development

"Pat has long been an inspiration to me. I watched how Pat made a space for Larry in her life long before she met him, and how she opened to love over time. Their love story is both inspiring and instructive."
~ Lisa Tener
Book Coach, Publishing Expert, Author, Speaker

"When your soul aches for happiness and a break from the divisiveness and duress of our world, this is a must-read book full of hope and love. These feelings permeate so deeply beneath the print that they spill over and take up residence in your heart. Tenderly and uniquely written from both the male and female perspective, the reader becomes not only enthralled with the journey of deep love upon which this couple has embarked but also feels guidance to envision their own spiritual and relational love journey. Begin that journey now."
~ Ruth McIntosh
Registered Nurse

"From a heart cast wide open after reading *It's Never Too Late for Love,* I dwell in awe in the grace of the inner essence of being in love that has been ignited. A higher perspective of how love looks feels and behaves in a shared love commitment is a powerful and significant prescription for its presence in the lives of all couples. Love is a choice that Pat and Larry have made as to their declaration and dedication to one another and all life. The most beautiful 'Love Story' told in their words and the spaces between their lines. An essential read and formula for life."
~ Kati Alexandra
Intuitive Reader, Facilitator of "Aloha Inner SPA"

"This book is a fascinating read on how to find your true love and have a great relationship with your mate. Also, this book is a powerful message on how to be a vessel of Love and to share that love with the world. I highly recommend it."
~ John Laney
Author of *You Are Incredible*

It's Never Too Late for Love

It's Never Too Late for Love

Manifesting Your Heart's Desire

Pat and Larry Burns

Sacred Life Publishers™
SacredLife.com
Printed in the United States of America

This book is dedicated to our six children,
nine grandchildren and the people in our lives
who we love because it is these people,
and the experiences shared with them,
that continually reinforce our commitment to love.
We believe that Love is all there is.

Contents

Foreword

On a Sunday morning new to Maui and three days married, I looked around the little church and wondered if any of my "yet to be met" friends were there. Belting out a spiritually optimistic song, my eyes and smile locked straight into the eyes and smile of a beautiful bright-eyed silver haired woman across the aisle from me. This was the kind of "soul spark" encounter that one knows is going to change your life for the better. When the service concluded this little woman and I just gravitated straight to each other and introduced ourselves. At that moment, Pat Hastings became my first friend on the island which was my new home. I am not alone in claiming that. There are a true handful of women who could all say the same thing. Pat just has that welcoming way.

As my friendship with Pat broadened, I came to know her beloved partner, Larry. Charming, humble, and kind, he was the thoughtful yin to her congenial yang. When they married, all who loved them celebrated the perfection of their love.

For the past several years it has been a privilege to watch the deepening and evolution of the Burns' marriage. Rather than a marriage to envy, they are creating a marriage to inspire. Pat and Larry exemplify the truth of real love. They are both similar and quite different. When one falls in love with a new partner in life's autumn chapter you are making a commitment to love another who has devoted decades to writing a life story of which you were not a part. Habits are entrenched. Preferences established. Communication styles and points of view the result of life experiences. When you fall in love in your fifties sixties, seventies, this is the stuff of true love.

When Pat and Larry decided to share the story of their love, I knew it was a gift of hope and encouragement to all of us. To those yet looking for love; Yes! This is a testament it can happen. To those questioning their partnership, this read will remind us that love isn't easy and is a choice every day. To those of you also living a life in love, this book will give you yet another story and reason to celebrate a life journey with another rich in the giving and receiving of the greatest gift of all.

I am grateful to Pat and Larry for sharing this story with me and with the world!

~ Kat Place, Maui 2020

Introduction

"It's Never Too Late for Love"
Manifesting Your Heart's Desire

Have you closed the door on your desires or given up hope to finding Love? Have you ever wondered? "I'm too old," "there are no good partners out there," or "am I going to be alone for the rest of my life?"

It's Never Too Late for Love is an inspirational and empowering story of a woman who had the courage and faith to follow her heart and manifest the desire of her heart. Pat left her home, family, career, friends, and community to find Love. She moved 5,000 miles across the ocean to the beautiful island of Maui, Hawaii. Pat met her soulmate and best friend, Larry, and they were married three years ago. They now live in a beautiful home overlooking the ocean on Maui.

Through the author's heartfelt experiences and wisdom, readers will find hope and inspiration to never give up on their dreams. Discover how you can manifest the desires of your heart and attract a committed loving relationship.

The book celebrates a couple's love and offers lessons learned along the path of consciousness. Accepting the gift of Love in our lives provides us with many opportunities to grow and evolve. Like the sun and rain, Love is a gift that is available to everyone regardless of race, religion, social, or economic status. Love does not discriminate and is available to everyone.

Each chapter illustrates an aspect of Pat and Larry's partnership. The couple shares how they navigate challenges guided by love, spirit, and grace. Through their experiences, discover how you can find the answers for your life and create a successful loving relationship. After each chapter, there are questions that invite you to go within and journal your responses.

The deep desires of your heart were placed there by Love. Embrace and honor these desires, they are the melody to the dance of life.

Chapter 1

Accepting the Opportunity

"In the middle of difficulty lies opportunity."
~ Albert Einstein

Pat and Larry:

I have been praying about writing a book with Larry about our "love story" and the power of Love Energy in our lives. It is my experience that it is *never too late to find true love,* no matter how old you are. I was in my late sixties and Larry was in his seventies when we met.

As I prayed about writing a book together, this is the message I received from Spirit:

> *"Say yes to be the light and love that I call you to be today. The world is awakening to the truth that we are all one and not separate from God. You know the truth and will share it with those I send to you. Do not be afraid of your light for it is my light shining through you. There is much darkness in the world that is now coming into the light. Although it looks like things in the world are deteriorating and people are very anxious and confused, it is my plan being played out. There is no need to be afraid because this has been planned by me and is the beginning of a great awakening."*

It is our belief that *Love is all there is.* It is all around us, within and without, and available to us right now. Each person has within them their own great Love story. Whether single or married, rich or poor, when you look at life through loving eyes, you are happy and have the only real wealth there is *Love* and the awareness of the light shining within your soul.

We are living one day at a time, trusting that God will provide, guide, and protect us every step of the way. God has a plan and all we have to do is say "yes" to that plan.

Pat and I share and discuss our spiritual journey often. We respect and encourage each other's growth and value each other's opinions. We have been praying about writing a book together and were waiting for signs that it was God's will.

I had a dream that was very meaningful, and I believe could be a sign from God that we were meant to write a book together. In my dream, Pat and I had a baby and I was trying to find a place to lay it down. The baby started to become cranky and unhappy. I remember thinking, "You are not going to be a cranky baby and the baby instantly became happy and peaceful." I believe the "baby" could be representing the book that we are writing and could be a nudge in that direction.

Writing a book together is definitely a stretch for me and I am completely out of my comfort zone. It's really difficult for me to share my spiritual journey of fifty years and private thoughts in public. I have learned, however, that Spirit will give us gentle nudges to get our attention. I think I'm feeling gentle nudges and I better listen.

I wonder, "why me?" What do I have to share with my fellow humans? I'm just a regular guy traveling my journey to the best of my ability. I have formed my own personal opinions about God, life, and spiritual beliefs. If by sharing my story I can help one person set himself or herself free of the bonds of guilt, despair, unworthiness, and fear, then I would consider the book a success.

During my morning walk and contemplation, I thought, "I want to accept every gift, every occasion in my life as something positive even if it frightens me or is asking me to stretch and leave my comfort zone. I will be open to all possibilities and see every gift as an opportunity."

My heart is full of gratitude for what Love has brought into my life. I am happy and look forward to walking this path of love with Pat as we grow spiritually as a couple and as individuals. We are given many opportunities every day to grow and become more conscious, and I'm excited to continue this journey and welcome all the opportunities that will arise.

We have seventy years of marital experience between the two of us before we met. Having arrived at a place of love, peace, joy, and gratitude, Pat and I are inspired to share our experiences with others who are being called to travel this journey of discovery and consciousness. We have learned some valuable lessons about love and relationships. Perhaps it will help you on your journey.

We believe that we are all connected, yet we all have different perspectives and that's *ok*. We understand there is no right way to reach the consciousness of *love*. We believe all roads lead to *love*, whatever your spiritual beliefs. We are not trying to change anyone's beliefs or say that our way is better than others. We are hoping our book encourages readers to seek the God who is Love, and they become familiar with the power and light that is given freely to everyone.

We are learning how to live our lives as vessels of Love. By becoming more conscious and being open to the energy and power of Love we are finding a life full of gratitude, peace, and joy. We are hoping there may be some gold nuggets that you find in our book that you can use on your spiritual journey. We are all connected. At the end of our journey we will all end up in the same place; Love will show us the way.

JOURNAL

Do I understand that every experience I encounter in life is a gift?

Do I see every challenge as an opportunity to grow and evolve?

Do I respect and value other's perspectives?

Chapter 2

A Modern-Day Love Story

"Being someone's first love may be great,
but to be the last is beyond perfect."
~ Linda Andrade Wheeler

Pat:

Many people have said to me, "When are you going to write your next book and the sequel to *Simply a Woman of Faith*? Friends have shared with us that our relationship is a model for them. They know it is attainable for them because of what they witness in our love relationship.

A friend shared her perspective on our relationship:

"To see the genuine love between Pat and Larry has helped me redefine what a love relationship can be. I have seen how they hold space for each other's highest and best expression of love to come through. The love, trust, and respect that they have for one another is a beacon for me in calling in my ideal soul mate and has helped me to understand and know that true love exists." Nancy Harris

It took me seven years to write my book, *Simply a Woman of Faith*. I was filled with fear and didn't believe in myself and didn't think anyone would read the book. I'm grateful to say that with the grace of God, I faced my fears, and *Simply a Woman of Faith* was published in 2007 and is an award winning book.

The last chapter in my book is about waiting for my soul mate to "show up." This is what I wrote:

"God's plan is perfect. I continue to pray and visualize my soul mate coming into my life. What I think about and thank about, I bring into my life. When I visualize, I materialize. I see in my mind's eye the end results and feel like it has already happened. I see my soul mate and I walking on the beach, having fun, and praying together. If God allows me to see it, I can trust he will bring it about. I'll have to write another book to share how God brings my soul mate into my life. I know it will be a wonderful story, no matter what, and it will be worth the wait."

My journey to meeting my soul mate started when a woman named, Ruth, invited me to be a speaker at her church. She was on the worship committee and had to organize ten spiritual speakers for the summer series. Ruth didn't know me but happened to be at another church service in the community and saw a flyer that I had left on the table. She said, "I felt your energy through your picture and decided to check out your website. Would you be interested in speaking at our church?"

Of course, I was thrilled and said, "Yes."

We met a few weeks before the talk to discuss what I would be speaking about and the logistics. I talked quite a bit about manifesting and the power of faith. When we were done, Ruth turned to me and said, "So Pat, what do you plan on manifesting next?" *I have no recall of saying* this, but Ruth remembers very clearly what happened. She said, "You put up your arms and said, 'I am going to live in Hawaii.'"

Ruth said, "I would love to introduce you to Ellen, who will be at the service this Sunday. Ellen lives on Maui and she is here visiting her daughter." After my talk on Sunday, Ruth brought Ellen over to introduce me to her. Ellen was a vivacious eighty-five-year-old woman. After some small talk, I said, "I have always wanted to visit Hawaii."

Ellen then whipped out a postcard of her condo, which overlooked the ocean, and said, "You can stay with me for as long as you want, and you can also use my car." I couldn't refuse her offer.

I visited Ellen for two weeks at Thanksgiving. I had never been away from my children for Thanksgiving and I had never traveled

5,000 miles for a vacation. We didn't know each other at all and here I was going to be staying with her in her home. Ellen invited me back the next year to stay in her condo for a month while she traveled. I jumped at the chance.

"Mother Maui" is magical, mystical, and beautiful. Not only is she beautiful with her flowers, mountains, and oceans, but there is a presence of Spirit that pulsated through my very being. I find it hard to put into words the feelings Maui evoked in me, other than love, peace, and joy. People smile and say hello and there is a feeling of oneness and aloha with all.

I fell in love with "Mother Maui". I knew in my Spirit that something very deep inside of me had shifted, but at the time, I didn't know what it was. When I left to go home, Ellen said to me, "Keep the vision of coming back." I did keep the vision and returned for one month the next year. It was then that I heard the "small, still voice of God" inviting me back to live there for six months.

I had to deal with all the voices in my head that said it was impossible to do. The strongest voice was, "Who do you think you are? You don't deserve to do something that extravagant." I had all kinds of questions like: How could I leave my family, friends, business, and community? Where would I live? Who would rent my condo in Rhode Island and where would the money come from?

I drove myself crazy and it wasn't until I got serious and ready that I finally went inside and asked myself the question, "What do I want?" How could God help me and go to work on my behalf if I wasn't clear about what I wanted?

After doing battle with God about why I couldn't possibly move to Maui and facing my fears, I finally surrendered and said "Yes." I went back home and told my family and friends that I was moving to Maui for six months. Of course, they were shocked and had all kinds of concerns and questions. All I knew for sure was that I was following my heart and trusting Spirit to do the rest.

When Spirit puts something on your heart that seems *impossible* and you "listen, trust, and *act*" doors open, almost miraculously. As I look back, I know it took a lot of courage and faith to trust myself and to trust it was the voice of Spirit and not just my own voice. I have had enough experience of listening and stepping out in faith to know it was true and that I could trust the voice within.

Within a few weeks of returning to Rhode Island, I found a woman who wanted to rent my condo, but I still didn't have a place to live when I arrived on Maui. I trusted something would "show up" and it did. Two weeks before arriving on Maui, I received a phone call from a friend inviting me to live with her and her husband in a two bedroom condo that they had just rented. I jumped at the chance and said, "Yes."

The condo overlooked the ocean and I paid 300 dollars a month. That is totally crazy because to rent a room on Maui for a night is over 200 dollars. I truly was in heaven and I learned how to relax and enjoy the journey. My plan was to continue my coaching practice and speaking engagements while I was on Maui. That was not God's plan. I heard very clearly, "I want you to learn *how to be*." I am so grateful that I listened because God's plan was so much better than mine.

When the six months ended, I knew my heart belonged on Maui and that I wanted to live there permanently. I had to deal with the same voices and fears again. After praying and meditating about it, I went back to Rhode Island and put my house up for sale. My house didn't sell, but I was able to rent it.

In September 2012, I moved back to Maui to live permanently and I have never been happier. It is amazing what happens when you listen to your heart and follow your inner guidance. Once I faced my fears and made the decision to move here, the energy and light of Love started to open doors, almost effortlessly. I found the perfect tenant for my condo in Rhode Island and was invited to live in a condo overlooking the ocean, for the unbelievable price of 300 dollars a month. I believed this was a confirmation from God that I had made the right decision. Thank you "Mother Maui" for inviting me to live in paradise and be a vessel of Love.

JOURNAL

When have I experienced God leading me in the past?

Do I have a dream that I'm afraid to follow?

Was there a time in my life where God helped me to do what seemed to be impossible?

Chapter 3

I Followed My Heart

"Don't let the mind tell your heart what to do.
Your mind gives us much to easily."
~ Anonymous

Pat:

When people ask me why I moved to Maui, I put my hand on my heart and answer, "I followed my heart and know I'm going to meet my soul mate." I didn't know how or when, but I knew in my heart that he was there waiting for me. Several years prior to moving to Maui, I attended a retreat called, "How to Have Your Heart's Desires Manifested". The desire of my heart was to meet my soul mate. Other than being kind, gentle, and trustworthy, my top priorities were that he be spiritual and that he liked to dance.

I was married for thirty years before getting a divorce in 1998. I was single for fifteen years before meeting my soul mate. During that time of being alone, I learned how to love and take care of myself. My trust in God deepened as I walked my faith journey.

I wasn't always patient waiting for my soul mate to "show up". I asked God, "What is wrong with me? Why haven't I met him yet? Are there any good men left?"

Shortly after I asked that question to God, I was shocked to receive this email in my inbox, and I didn't know who it was from. This is what it said:

Love Letter From GOD

Everyone longs to give themselves completely to someone—to have a deep soul relationship with another, to be loved thoroughly and exclusively. But God says:

"No, not until you are satisfied, fulfilled, and content with being loved by me alone. I love you my child and until you discover that only in Me is your satisfaction to be found, you will not be capable of the *perfect relationship* that I have planned for you. You will never be united with another until you are united with me, exclusive of any other longings or desires. I want you to stop wishing, planning, and allow me to give you the most thrilling plan existing, one that you cannot imagine. I want you to have the BEST. Please allow me to bring it to you. You just keep watching, learning, and listening to the things I tell you. *You must wait.* And then you will be *ready. I will surprise you with a love that is far more wonderful than you could ever dream of.*

Know that I love you utterly, I am God. Believe it and be satisfied."

Love, God

This is what I did while waiting for my soulmate to manifest:

- I put God first through daily prayer and meditation.
- I learned to love and appreciate myself.
- I gave myself what I needed, instead of looking outside for someone to give it to me.
- I learned how to *be* and relax.
- I opened my heart to *receive* Love.
- I did affirmations daily and made a picture book of what I wanted to manifest.

I had lived on Maui for a few months when I attended a dance at the Senior Center with my friends. As expected, there were more women than men and if you wanted to dance, you had to be brave and ask a man to dance. Otherwise, you would sit all night and not dance at all. I asked a man to dance who was tall, good looking with beautiful blue eyes and grey hair. His name was Larry. He was friendly and polite and asked, "Where do you live?"

I responded, "I just moved to Maui a couple of months ago and I grew up in New York."

He smiled, "I'm from Connecticut and have lived on the island for seven years."

Since I loved to dance, I attended ballroom dances on Saturday nights. I remember holding my breath the first time I walked into the dance alone and not knowing anyone. I did it because if I wanted to meet my soul mate, I had to go where the men were. I was happy to see Larry there from the Senior Center and asked him to dance. He shared he was recently divorced. I remember clearly one night after Larry and I danced, a conversation I started with him. He said something about *love*. My heart definitely skipped a beat and I wanted to know more about this man. He asked me, "Would you like to go for a walk with me sometime?"

I said, "Yes, that would be lovely." Although I didn't feel a physical attraction to him, I was interested in getting to know him. He appeared to be a kind gentleman. I made it clear to him that I wasn't interested in a romantic relationship and he accepted that I just wanted to be friends.

Larry and I started to take walks by the ocean and went to lunch weekly. In no time, we became best friends and called each other nightly to see how our day went. I called him, "Mr. Magnificent". I trusted him and knew he was there for me whenever I needed him. We went deep fast and shared what was important to us, our values, and our spiritual beliefs. We were out to breakfast with a friend who was a doctor when Larry felt ill and was about to faint. I will never forget when he looked at me and said, "Don't ever forget how much I love you."

Larry moved to Maui from Connecticut in 2007. He had very good friends that moved to Maui from Connecticut in 2003 that he visited often. He shared with me, "From the moment I walked off the plane, Maui embraced me and has never let me go. The last time I visited my friends in February 2006, I was at the airport and ready to depart when I made the decision that I had to move to Maui. I felt so sad leaving and didn't want to leave."

He shared, "Maui has been the perfect fit for me, and I absolutely love living here. The weather is perfect, the local people are fantastic and openly practice *ALOHA*. There have been some challenging times (my marriage of nineteen years ended, and I had some health issues) but mostly it has been terrific."

My girlfriends knew I wanted to meet my soul mate and asked me often, "Pat, what is wrong with Larry, you are always talking about him and he is so nice?"

I said, "We are best friends, but I don't have a physical attraction toward him." You just can't make that happen.

Larry started to date another woman and they became quite serious. I often helped him to process his feelings and affirmed him for his behaviors. The relationship didn't work out. They broke up and I was there to help him move through his grief.

It was only a few weeks after they broke up that I realized that I had "feelings" for Larry. He joined me for the Easter Sunday celebration at Unity Church. I was so touched when he gave me a beautiful white flower lei right before the service. I remember during the service, praying, "God, open my heart if Larry is my soul mate."

I was just beginning to have some romantic stirrings towards him after being best friends for two years. I believe it was that prayer that awakened me to the reality of love right before my eyes. I also knew that it wasn't God's timing until that very moment that my heart opened. Although we were best friends and had built our relationship on trust and respect, we each had some inner work to do before we moved to the next level of our journey together.

I was beside myself and afraid to tell him that I had *feelings* for him. We had such a good relationship as friends, and I didn't want to destroy that. I called him and invited him to come over. When he stopped by, I said, "I have a bomb to drop." He looked surprised but listened intently. "I have *feelings* for you."

He looked shocked. He had no idea that was coming and said, "Let's see what happens."

A few days later, we were taking a walk on the beach and holding hands when I shared with him, "I'm afraid to kiss you." He stopped and turned me toward him and gently kissed me on the mouth. I said, "Well, that wasn't so bad." Within a few weeks, we were a couple and in love.

JOURNAL

Do I know how to listen and follow my heart and intuition?

When was the last time I trusted Love to show me the way?

Was there a time in my life when I followed my heart, even though it didn't make sense?

Chapter 4

Love

*"Love is the only force capable of transforming
an enemy into a friend."*
~ Martin Luther King, Jr.

Larry:

During my spiritual journey of the last fifty years, I have developed perspectives that to some would appear to be different than most. As I am evolving, my beliefs and perspectives will change. I am not suggesting that one should adopt my philosophy. I share it with you so that you may understand better what I'm referring to in my story.

Have you ever considered the possibility that "Love" is God? What a wonderful revelation! Love is the most powerful energy known to humankind, stronger than hate, violence, or natural disasters. Think of the possibilities; Love doesn't judge, is forgiving, patient, kind, flexible, and available to all just like the sun that shines and the rain that falls. There is no discrimination; Love is available to everyone, it doesn't have to be earned, it is given freely for the asking. Love always guides, provides, and protects.

I believe that what the world needs now is Love Consciousness. I see Love Consciousness as knowing, accepting, and trusting that Love is available to all humankind, trusting that the power, energy, and light of Love is what our world is being called to accept, and when we do our world will become the heaven on earth it was meant to be.

I remember when I first became conscious that the power and energy of Love were available to me without having to earn it or be worthy of it, I began to ask for Love's help in my daily experiences. For example: going to the dentist or doctors used to be incredibly stressful for me. As I walked towards their office my heart would start to race and I could feel my blood pressure go up. Love Consciousness helped me to understand that I was choosing to fear instead of Love. I changed my perspective and started to choose Love. As I walked towards the dentist or doctor's office, I began saying over and over to myself, "I choose Love, I choose Love." My stress disappeared, and I became calm and fearless. I do this now in every stressful situation that arises in my life. Love has never let me down.

This is the God I have in my life and you can too. When I use the word Love in this book please understand, I use it synonymously with the word God.

Every heart and soul has the capacity to receive and share Love. I believe that we are all called to be vessels of Love, and to the extent that we can accept this, it will change the world. It's my goal to not allow fear to have power in my life anymore. I bring everything to Love because that is where the power is, and Love has never failed me. The more that I allow myself to be a vessel of Love, the more Love comes into my life.

While on my spiritual journey, I struggled for years with the concept of becoming a "vessel of Love". I knew in my heart and soul that this was the direction I was being encouraged to take. The more I contemplated this, the more I realized it would not be popular or an easy path for me. Unfortunately, being a vessel of Love is not seen as being very "masculine" in our society.

I felt afraid of being judged and realized my ego was trying to make me feel "less than". With Pat's encouragement and support, I felt safe to reveal this part of my heart that I had hidden for years and was reluctant to share with others. This is a perfect example of how love, respect, and trust are the foundation of our relationship and enabled me to stop hiding what was important to me.

Since I have become more conscious, my priority is to be a vessel of Love wherever I go. I'm aware that in every situation, I'm given the opportunity to choose either Love or fear. As I evolve, my goal is to always choose Love. My spiritual journey is similar to Pat's in that we both desire to be vessels of Love in whatever we do and wherever we go. This is a perfect opportunity to develop and deepen our love relationship.

Here are some of the challenges that surfaced as I began to grow and evolve: *impatience, anger, unkindness, unconsciousness, ego, selfishness, fear, judging others, etc.*

As I address these areas in my life, I become a better person and a better husband.

By becoming more conscious, I am learning *trust, patience, kindness, flexibility, fearlessness, generosity, unselfishness, openness to the power and energy of Love.*

I don't do these things perfectly. That's not the point, we do not have to be perfect to be vessels of Love. Once we become conscious that we are being called to be a vessel of Love, it becomes a priority in our lives. It's been wonderful to discover that the power and energy of Love have always been available to me and I am worthy of that gift. Love has never let me down. I'm sure I will continue with Love's help to evolve until I leave this form.

What if we took a moment to imagine that we chose this life adventure because "Love" wanted to experience itself as form? We were given the opportunity to choose to become Love in Form.

I don't believe there is a heaven up in the sky somewhere that we go to when we die or a God that is waiting to judge and condemn us. I believe that we are all spirits, connected through Love/God. I believe that when we transcend from our form, we will return from whence we came and reconnect as cells in the body of Love. Where we will experience a depth of Love that you can't imagine.

As I contemplated this, I wondered what my life would look like and how my life would change if I honestly endeavored to be a vessel of Love. I would have to first believe that my reason for walking this journey in form is *"to be a vessel of Love."*

As a vessel of Love, I would recognize and confront my ego. I would know that the more I love myself, the more I could love others and learn how to forgive and love those who have hurt me. I would stop making my life so busy and stressful. I would stop thinking that I'm unworthy to be a vessel of Love.

As a vessel of Love, I would be open to the energy and light of Love and allow Love to lead me. I would know that Love is like the sun, which shines its light on everyone and doesn't discriminate. I would be accepting and not judge others. I would choose Love over fear.

JOURNAL

What keeps me from being a vessel of Love?

What are the challenges I might experience being a vessel of Love?

How would my life change if I honesty endeavored to be a vessel of Love?

Chapter 5

I Can Have It All

"Love is two human hearts coming together
and knowing together they are ONE"
~ Linda Andrade Wheeler

Larry:

I remember saying to Pat before she told me she had romantic feelings for me, "We are lucky we're not in a romantic relationship because it would probably destroy this great friendship we have." We had been best friends for two years and had formed a bond of trust and appreciation for each other that few people have.

When Pat said she had romantic feelings for me, a lot of my "head" stuff popped up. I asked myself, "Do I want to risk a wonderful friendship and allow myself to see this relationship in a different way? I wondered if I would get hurt, if it would last, or can I trust Love?" Fear wasn't far behind.

I had also just ended a relationship that I thought was the best I ever had but ended up with me being blindsided and hurt. I asked myself, "Do I want to risk that again? How could I trust again? Isn't it too soon to start another relationship?"

My response to Pat was, "Let's see what happens." Since we already had such a great relationship and I really trusted her, I was gradually able to face my fears, get out of my head and let my heart receive the love that was being offered to me. I let my heart lead, trusted Love, let go of fear, and all the negative thoughts and doubts that would have sabotaged this opportunity for a love relationship.

I'm thankful to Love (God) for helping me to forgive, heal, and move on so I could accept this wonderful gift that Pat is in my life. I always knew I could have it all, and now I do.

Being in a love relationship brings up my insecurities and where I need to change and grow. It takes a tremendous amount of courage in a relationship to put your heart out there unprotected and take a chance and allow Love to lead the way.

Some people may think one way to preserve the relationship we have with ourselves is to hold back in a love relationship. If we hold back and there is a breakup we won't get hurt and we still have our self. I'm not sure how to do that and still have a healthy love relationship. Holding back is a tactic I've used when I felt afraid and allowed fear to call the shots in a relationship. I believe it's quite courageous to put yourself out there and allow yourself to love and be loved again.

I'm beginning to understand that for most of my life, I looked outside of myself to find the answers. By looking inside, I found the emptiness and allowed Love to fill it. If we don't love ourselves and allow Love to show us how important we are and how much Love wants to lavish itself upon us, we will never be able to have a healthy love relationship with someone else.

During the two years of my friendship with Pat, she recognized that I had a difficult time accepting compliments or gifts from others. While Pat and I were discussing the reasons why it's difficult to receive compliments and positive attention, I became aware of how Love energy works by teaching us through our experiences.

A thought occurred to me that when I receive a compliment or receive positive feedback from another, I act like a turtle. A turtle often presents itself dozing on a rock near a pond or around a shoreline with its head out enjoying the sun. Then as you approach the turtle, it immediately pulls its head in for protection. I'm beginning to understand that is what I've done when someone offers me a compliment or responds to something I've done in a positive manner.

I pull back to protect myself because I'm afraid they will discover the real me, not the one they admire. If they knew what I struggle with each day to become that person they admire, they would have never offered me a compliment. If they could see my struggle with my ego and fear, they wouldn't be giving me compliments.

Then the ego tries to convince me that the person giving me a compliment really didn't mean what they said. They are just trying to be nice or perhaps they want something from me. I talk and write a lot about love, kindness, and forgiveness and people have said to me, "That's easy for you to do." I look at them in astonishment, smile, and slowly shake my head. Why would it be easier for me to do?

It seems my mindset in the past has been that I have to say it, write it, and practice it perfectly before I can take credit for it. Love/God is showing me that this is ridiculous. Trying to be perfect is an old belief that no longer serves me and never has.

When a person gives me a compliment now, I thank them. I'm choosing to believe that I have touched them, they appreciate it and they want me to know that. I hear Love saying to me, "Don't pull your head back like a turtle, accept the gift and compliment, live in the moment, and enjoy the experience." I'm learning to do that.

Pat helped me to recognize that I have some exceptionally good qualities. She has always been free with her compliments and support. She suggested that it was not being conceited or selfish to claim them for myself. I think I've come a long way and I'm in a much better place now than when we met. I feel the energy and light of Love in my life and my tank is full.

When our vehicles get low on fuel, we go to the gas station and fill our tanks. When our love tanks are low or empty it could be a sign that we are not loving ourselves enough. Maybe we've been under too much stress lately or working long hours or have gone through a difficult experience. Is it time for a "Love check"? It sounds like your battery is low and your love tank is empty. It could be a signal to take some love time for yourself. Do something fun, spend some quality time with loved ones, or perhaps just get some rest.

When my love tank is full and I am loving myself, I can share that love with others by offering acts of kindness and support. When I am kind or loving to another person, I contribute to filling their love tank and my love tank also benefits from that experience. I endeavor to be a loving and caring soul, but many times, I come up short. I tend to remember those times more than the times I succeed.

JOURNAL

Do I look outside for my answers, rather than go within?

How do I react when I have been hurt in a relationship?

Do I have to do things perfectly to feel worthy of Love?

Chapter 6

The Desire of My Heart

"What your heart desires is not too good to be true.
It is good enough to be true."
~ Alan Cohen

Pat:

Larry and I have the same values, priorities, and outlook on life. Spirituality is particularly important to Larry, as it is to me. We have both been on the spiritual path for many years before we met. When we became a couple, Larry made it very clear to me that he didn't have any interest in getting married again, as he had already been divorced twice. He was fine with a committed relationship, but not marriage. In fact, we had a commitment ceremony that was unbelievably beautiful.

Although marriage was the desire of my heart, I accepted Larry not wanting to get married again. We discussed the pros and cons of getting married and Larry was still very strong in his opinion. He said, "We have such a great relationship now and I am totally committed to you. I don't know why we need to get married."

All I needed to do was be patient, let go, wait, keep my mouth shut, and trust Spirit. With the grace of God, I kept my mouth shut (which was not an easy task) and Spirit changed Larry's heart about getting married.

When I prayed about it, Spirit assured me that the desire of my heart to be married would be fulfilled. Spirit said,

"Trust in my timing and relax. I am working in Larry's heart. This is my plan for you, and nothing can stop it. You don't have to do anything but continue to love and be."

25

Thank you for making me *ready!* Waiting for fifteen years for Larry has not been easy, but it has been worth the wait. Truly, *I have been surprised with a Love that is far more wonderful than I could have ever imagined.* My heart is full of gratitude for all Spirit has done in my life and it continues to get better and better.

I asked Larry to go on a cruise with me for my seventieth birthday. Through the grace of God, I felt peaceful and surrendered when Larry said he didn't want to go on the cruise. I had accepted that it wasn't God's will and was able to let it go. Through a series of unrelated events, I started to think about it again.

A friend asked me, "What do you really want to do for your birthday?"

I said, "I don't know." At that point, I really didn't know what I wanted because I had accepted that I wasn't going and had let it go.

I felt conflicted and went within to ask myself some questions, "Am I being selfish and wanting my own way? Is this desire to celebrate my birthday on a cruise from God? Will I be creating problems in our relationship? Am I denying myself something that I really want that is important to me?"

When I went to bed that night, I asked God for a dream to help me discern what was my highest good. As I worked with the dream, I realized I did want to go on a cruise and that I wasn't being honest with myself or Larry.

I asked myself how often in my life did I stay stuck (and didn't get what I wanted) because I said, "I don't know what I want?" In my former marriage, it was easier to not speak up because I didn't want to rock the boat. I also wouldn't be disappointed if I just denied my needs and desires and kept my mouth shut. This clearly doesn't work for me anymore.

Once I admitted that this is what I really wanted to do for my birthday, I made the decision to go on the cruise by myself. Larry didn't want to go because he had already been on that Hawaiian cruise. I trusted that the money would show up as it had so many times in the past when God led me to step out in faith. I was listening to my heart and not my head which was telling me why it wouldn't work, and I couldn't go.

I contacted Norwegian Cruise Line again to discuss the Hawaiian island cruise. To my delight and surprise, the agent informed me that there was a significant (1,300 dollar) discount for people who lived in Hawaii. I could afford this cruise if I went alone or if Larry joined me.

When Larry came home that afternoon, I shared with him what was going on and the dream I had worked with. I said, "This is what I really want to do for my birthday. I would love for you to join me, but I am fine going by myself if you choose not to go." When we trust God and follow our hearts, all things work for the good and there is peace in our hearts. I am grateful to be living in God's perfect will for me.

JOURNAL

Do I know what I want?

Am I able to wait patiently and trust God's timing?

What is the desire of my heart?

Chapter 7

The Cruise

"I want to feel the rhythm of my soul and dance to its music."
~ Linda Andrade Wheeler

Larry:

The energy of Love is always calling us to greater consciousness, encouraging us to grow by recognizing our fears and letting them go. From my experience, sometimes that can be uncomfortable and difficult. What's important to me is that I continue my journey by not allowing fear to determine which direction I go. I'm learning to choose Love and not allow fear to run my life.

Pat invited me to go on a cruise with her for her seventieth birthday. Initially, I said, "If you really want me to go, I will go with you." As I thought more about it, I said, "No, I really don't want to go." She understood and affirmed me for saying no, which had been difficult for me in the past. She didn't want me to go if I didn't really want to.

I was relieved and thought the issue was closed. A week later, she decided to go by herself, regardless of the expense. She invited me to join her but said she would go either way. I knew then that this was important to her and I really didn't want her to go alone.

I am *choosing* to see this as an opportunity to make a loving choice for Pat and have a fun time together, regardless of where the cruise is going. I realized how happy I am to have her in my life to experience these adventures together.

Being in a relationship is like a dance. When you are dancing and moving to the beat and rhythm of the music and you're in sync with one another, it's a wonderful experience. I think being in a relationship is about trying to incorporate the beat and rhythm of each other's personalities, perspectives, wishes, and desires. When we accomplish this through love, compassion, generosity, and flexibility, it becomes a wonderful experience.

Being in a relationship is not always about *me*. Sometimes, it's about *us* and doing things I may not want to do. It could be an opportunity to be understanding of the needs of my partner. When Pat suggests that we do something out of the ordinary that will stretch me, my default seems to be *no thank you!* She has learned to plant the seed, back off and let me think about it. Sometimes, after I think about the suggestion for a while, I come around.

Since she was really excited about the cruise, I agreed to go, even though I was not as enthusiastic as she was. I was happy to accompany her and promised her, "I would be positive and supportive." I looked forward to having a great time with her.

It was a terrific cruise and we had a fabulous time. Pat had been trying to expand her ability to love and be loved. Since she was already such a loving person, I wondered how she would be able to do that. We spent a lot of time together talking and being present to one another with kindness and love. I thought we had a very special relationship and from my perspective, it couldn't get any better.

Love knows better. As we remained open with an attitude of gratitude, things started to happen and we both started to expand, and the feeling of wellness and love was incredible. It is our desire to become the best vessels of Love we can be. I believe my heart is my vessel, and to the extent that I open my heart, it will be filled with the energy and light of Love.

As I witnessed Pat confront some issues that had been major walls in her life for many years, her expansion was incredible. She was able to accept and allow her heart to receive the continuing gift of Love. Her heart expanded to overflowing and I was the recipient of that overflowing fountain of love.

In turn, my response to her expansion was that my heart expanded to receive all the Love energy and light that was being offered to me. I was able to love her more deeply and give to her in a way that I hadn't been able to respond before.

Not only did I feel more connected to Pat, but I felt connected to every soul on the ship. I was aware of how hard everyone worked to make this cruise a wonderful experience for the guests (cabin steward, wait staff, kitchen workers, servers, and cooks). I was free with compliments and appreciation. It was fantastic to see their eyes light up when I mentioned what a good job they were doing or how much I appreciated their hard work.

This cruise experience has confirmed for me that Love is never done giving, all we need to do is be open to it, and our vessels will be filled to overflowing. Remember: "Love in your heart is not put there to stay. Love is not love until you give it away." The more we give the more we receive.

Things were going great for us on the cruise. Pat was facing her fears and showing how courageous she was by opening up to a greater deeper gift of Love. We were living in the energy and light of gratitude and appreciation. I discovered that when we can recognize that energy and accept it, miracles happen. I was feeling more loved and accepted than I have ever been before.

After we returned from the cruise the small, still voice of "Love/God" kept working on me, reminding me of how much I loved and respected Pat. I knew that getting married would be a wonderful gift I could give her. I started having thoughts that perhaps "marriage would not be so bad." I began to realize on a deeper level what a "gift" Pat was in my life. Love kept giving me these gentle nudges towards marriage until I finally said, "O.K. I will ask her to marry me."

You may be wondering why I changed my mind about marriage after being so against it. I don't know if I can really explain the shift that led me to want to marry Pat. I know that if Pat had nagged or pushed me to marry her, I would probably not have experienced the "shift" that occurred. Sometimes when the energy of Love is present, things happen, and we can't explain why or how.

I still didn't feel marriage would change my commitment to Pat in any way or that it would protect our relationship from dissolving. I think some people feel marriage will give them added security about a relationship not ending. I think that is a false sense of security.

In following my heart, I concluded that our marriage is in God's plan and for our highest good. I guess that's a pretty good reason for getting married. Plus, the fact that our relationship is over the top and so beneficial to both of us. I look forward to spending the rest of my life with Pat.

I said nothing to anyone about what I was doing while I searched for an engagement ring to surprise her. The rest is history.

JOURNAL

Am I open to the gift of Love by facing my fears?

Am I able to open my heart and receive the gift of Love?

How has Love/God nudged me in the past and have I listened?

Chapter 8

You Are My Queen, I Am Your King

"Any home can be a castle when the king and queen are in love."
~ Anonymous

Pat:

It is not easy to surprise me. I am very intuitive and like to know everything going on around me. During prayer and meditation two days before Larry proposed to me, I received a message from Spirit that said, *"Prepare yourself for new things coming into your life and you will be surprised."*

I wasn't *prepared* and my life was about to change in a big way.

I invited my girlfriends over for our annual Christmas get together dinner. My friend, Kati, gifted me with a beautiful gold queen's crown. My favorite cup that I drink from every morning says, "I am the queen." A queen leads and loves from her heart. She is able to receive love and knows what she wants. She is not afraid to share her feelings or set her boundaries. She trusts all is in divine order.

Larry was in the den watching TV and the girls wanted to say hello and show him my new crown. We all pranced in and I put the crown on my head and then put it on Larry's head and said, "You are my king." It was quite funny, and we all had a good laugh.

I had no idea that Larry was planning to ask me to marry him. He had asked Spirit to lead him and was waiting for the right time to propose to me and give me the ring. When Kati gave me the crown, he knew it was his sign to propose to me.

My girlfriends and I left the den to continue our festivities. Five minutes later, Larry came into the living room and stood in front of me and said, "Please come over here and sit down."

I jokingly remarked, "He's going to ask me to marry him—yeah right!"

He stood before me and said, "You are my queen and I am your king; would you like to make it permanent and legal?" He then got on one knee and presented me with a beautiful diamond ring that he pulled out of his pocket.

I was in total shock and could hardly talk as my jaw dropped to the ground. I was in such a daze that I asked him, "Are you really asking me to marry you?" Of course, my girlfriends were going crazy as they witnessed this beautiful gift of our love in action.

After the women left, Larry shared with me, "Because of our amazing experience on the cruise, I began to think that marriage may not be such a bad idea. I knew that it was the desire of your heart, although you never did anything to try to get me to change my mind or push the matter."

It is my belief that God gives us the desires of our hearts. I trusted and waited for fifteen years as I grew and evolved to the place where I could accept the gift of my soulmate coming into my life. During that time, I learned how to love myself first. There are times in our lives when we ask God for something, but we are not ready for it to manifest. We must wait, trust, and be patient until we can accept and appreciate the gift of Love in our lives. God's timing is always perfect. God is still writing our Love story as two hearts are united in Love.

JOURNAL

Am I ready to manifest my soulmate?

What do I want to manifest from my heart?

When has God surprised me?

Am I able to love myself first?

Chapter 9

Planning a Wedding

"We make plans and God laughs."
~ Anonymous

Pat:

It's hard to believe that at age seventy, I was planning a wedding. As Larry's gift to me, he gave me free rein to choose what I wanted as far as decorating, songs, invitations, etc. I loved being a *bride*. I'm having fun and enjoying every moment of it. Right from the start, Larry and I both affirmed that everything would flow with peace, ease, and grace because we knew weddings could be very stressful and we work hard at avoiding stress in our lives. I found the perfect wedding dress. It was the first one I tried on and it fit me to a tee. I felt like Cinderella with my new sparkly diamond sandals.

My Maid of Honor, Kati, and I created the wedding invitations and we just loved them. I showed the invitation to a friend and she said, "I will use this as a vision board for what I want to attract into my life."

We were married five months later. Our plan was to get married in a beautiful little Hawaiian church on Maui with a reception to follow at Cafe Ole. Invitations were done and ready to be sent out when I received an email from the minister, "Pat, I am so sorry, but the church is no longer available for your wedding. The board just informed me there was a prior event that involved all the churches in Hawaii coming here that day. Can we do it another day?"

I would say that not having a church to get married in is a big change of plans! As I read the email to Larry, we looked at one another in shock and said, "OK, now what?" In the past, we may have gone into a panic, felt angry, and indignant that this happened to us. Instead, we accepted it and knew that it was going to work out for our highest good. We were given an opportunity to trust and practice what we believe.

We discussed a few different options and called some other churches in the area, but to no avail. Then the idea came into my mind, "Why not get married in our beautiful home?" We can turn our home into a sacred sanctuary filled with love, friends, and beautiful flowers.

We were married in our home on the lanai, overlooking the ocean. Our home was transformed into a beautiful sanctuary with colorful red and yellow Hawaiian flowers and pink rose petals were strewn across the floor.

My daughter, Mary, walked me up the aisle to greet my beloved, Larry, waiting for me on our lanai with the rest of our friends. My grandson, Herbie, was the ring bearer. It was a gorgeous setting as our lanai overlooks the ocean and the pink and white Plumeria trees were in full bloom. I truly felt like I was royalty with my beautiful lei and haiku (headpiece) and the most grateful and happiest woman alive.

Larry wore a white Hawaiian shirt and white pants and looked like a knight in shining armor. He looked so handsome that he took my breath away. I had waited for this sacred moment for so long and now it was here. When the service began, I looked out into the faces of our smiling friends with tears rolling down their cheeks. I knew Spirit was present and with us. My daughter, Mary, surprised me by taking a video of the ceremony so my children and grandchildren were able to be present. What a special gift that was knowing they were celebrating with us.

The reception was truly a "Love Fest". I believe that all of life can be a Love Fest! We are all beings of Love and light and are invited to dance and play in the fields of the lord. Our reception was a powerful reminder of how God fills our lives with Love if we allow it.

After thanking all of our friends for all of their help, Larry said grace before the meal and said, "Our purpose is to love, laugh, and let our lights shine." We had a delicious meal, drank wine, danced, and had a great time.

JOURNAL

How do I react when there is a change of plans?

Am I able to go with the flow and trust?

Chapter 10

The Wedding

"Love is like a friendship caught on fire."
~ Jeremy Taylor

Larry:

May 13, 2017 dawned sunny and beautiful with white and pink plumeria trees in full bloom. I felt excited and a little nervous. This was the day Pat and I were going to tie the knot. Since the ceremony was taking place in our home the energy was high with the anticipation of the wedding.

As the guests started to arrive, I felt a kind of peace and calm come over me. It felt good to have all our friends gather to witness our wedding. It was such a joy for me to feel all that Love energy that was radiating through everyone as I greeted them.

Reverend Kamuela Rodrigues, our Hawaiian minister, had arrived and we were almost ready to start the ceremony. I felt nervous and anxious waiting on our lanai with all our guests for my bride to arrive. The minister asked, "May I please have the marriage license?" I looked at him with a deer in the headlight look.

I completely forgot about the marriage license and had no idea where we put it. I immediately called Pat (who was getting dressed at her friend's house) and anxiously asked, "Where is the license, we can't get married if we don't have it."

She calmly said, "Look in the file box, I think it's there." Sure enough, it was there and thank goodness the ceremony was able to proceed.

When I saw Pat approaching and walking down the aisle with her beautiful smile and sparkly blue eyes, I felt so proud and happy to be joining her in this beautiful experience that would make us husband and wife. She looked so beautiful it took my breath away.

There was a part of the ceremony that I had really been dreading. We had written our own vows that we would recite to one another. I have always had a difficult time showing my emotions. I felt embarrassed and tried to hold them back. For as long as I can remember, my family has always been very emotional, and we cried at the drop of a hat.

The truth is I am a very emotional person. It was very difficult for me to recite my vows to Pat without choking up and blubbering in front of all our guests. Once I got through this, the rest of the ceremony went smoothly, and I relaxed and enjoyed myself.

A friend of ours shared,

> *"I was so touched when I witnessed Larry allowing himself to be emotional. It was very healing to see the emotion expressed between the two of them. To see Larry well up with tears as he said his vows, awakened in me that men can be truly sensitive and loving. It imprinted in my heart the desire to attract a man who is willing to be both vulnerable and strong. This is not something I have experienced much of, but now I know it is available."*

Our marriage ceremony was an expression of our love for one another. This Love is available to all of us as a pure gift when we are open to see the goodness and light within another human being. It is available to you right now and is a perfectly natural response when you realize that whomever you are being present with is a *being of light* who deserves to be loved, cherished, and honored.

We had a wonderful reception enjoying our family and friends, sharing love, dance, laughter, and joy.

JOURNAL

Do I want to attract a partner who is both strong and vulnerable?

Do I have a difficult time showing my emotions?

Chapter 11

Asking for What You Want and Need

"Let us allow LOVE to be the music in our cosmic dance."
~ Anonymous

Pat:

Larry celebrated his eightieth birthday with thirty-five friends and family at our home. What a beautiful day of love, peace, and joy. The love just *flowed*.

One of the reasons I felt so peaceful was that I've learned to ask for what I need. I asked a friend to come over a couple of days before the party and we discussed everything, as well as set up tables and figured out where the food was going to be placed. It was such a blessing to not have to do it all by myself.

I remember an incident years ago with my ex-husband. We were having company, and he was laying on the couch reading the paper, while I was racing around the house trying to get ready. I felt angry and resentful that he wasn't helping, and I was doing everything. I finally snapped and said something to him. I will never forget his remark, "Why didn't you just ask me for help?"

I never thought to ask him for help. The lesson for me was that *I expected him to read my mind.* Of course, we could say he should have known and perhaps he could have been more aware, but he wasn't. Expecting someone to read my mind and know what I need is setting myself up for trouble.

Why is it so hard to ask for help?

- We don't want to be rejected.
- We don't want to bother others.
- We may be afraid of what will be asked of us.

- We think we should know what to do.
- We don't want to appear weak, needy, incompetent.
- We may not think our needs are important.

Asking for help is *not* a sign of weakness, but a sign of *strength*. If I hadn't asked for help and gone into therapy many years ago when I needed it, I would not be who and where I am today.

It's important to let go of the "outcome" when we ask for what we want and need. We have to be prepared for a *no* and not hold a resentment if we do get a no. Others have a right to say no when it's not good for them.

Do you think that asking for what you want or need makes you feel less than? Thinking this is an old belief that is born out of a lack of respect and love for yourself. A lack of self-respect can lead to feelings of unworthiness, or less important than others, and cause you to subordinate your own needs and not ask for what you want.

Like many women, I wasn't taught how to be assertive and ask for what I wanted. I often used the silent treatment or dropped hints and then expected my loved ones to read my mind. I then became resentful if my needs weren't met. I have learned to be assertive and practice boldness when the opportunity arises. It is not always comfortable, and I feel vulnerable asking sometimes, but I do it anyway because I love myself and know my needs are important.

I love the book *The 5 Love Languages* by Gary Chapman. It is very helpful in a love relationship to know each other's love language and to honor that for one another. They are words of affirmation, quality time together, acts of service, physical touch, and gifts.

Larry and I have the same first love language and that is physical touch. It is easy for us to show our love for one another through touch. A close second for me is gifts. It doesn't have to be anything big or expensive. It can be a card or a flower, something that lets me know I am thought about and loved. I love to send cards and give gifts for no reason at all.

I know, without a doubt, that Larry loves me by the way he treats and respects me. I could not ask for a better partner and know we are perfectly matched. Many months ago, Larry and I had a conversation about my love language of gifts. He heard me and responded in kind.

I am thrilled when I receive a card in the mail, or when he picks me a flower on his way home. He even bought some cards to have in the house to give me when he wanted to. Because this is not his love language, he forgets that it is important to me. It's not on his mind until I bring it up to him.

When I became aware that it had been a while since I received a gift from Larry, I was tempted to drop a hint about how much I love flowers, instead of being honest with him. I decided to be honest and tell him what my needs were. I have learned that I must *honor* my love language and that it is important to me. I wasn't going to judge it and tell myself I was selfish or wrong for wanting this from Larry. Certainly, Larry had a choice to hear me or ignore me.

When I brought it up to him, he was defensive at first. He said something like, "Look at all the ways I love you already." He was absolutely right; he does love me in so many beautiful ways. Larry decided to listen to me and the next day I found a card with a poem in it on my pillow.

I texted him and said, "You made my day. I just got the card and poem and loved it. Thank you for hearing me."

Asking for What You Want and Need

Larry:

I'm not sure why, but I'm not particularly good at asking for help or for what I need. I think that asking for help implies that I have failed to accomplish the challenge presented to me and it makes me feel less than. I also do not like to bother people and I feel embarrassed asking for help.

When Pat broke her shoulder a few months ago, friends began calling and asking her how they could help. Pat had no problem asking them to donate some meals if they wanted to. When she told me she asked for meals I replied, "Oh man, why did you do that? We have plenty of food, do we really need friends to bring us food?" I felt embarrassed and ashamed that we had asked for food.

Pat's reply was, "I can't cook with my broken shoulder and you don't like to cook. You are very busy now doing everything around the house and taking care of me. You're in your eighty-second year and you just can't do everything."

Wow! Men and women are so different from one another. I wonder sometimes how we can ever have a lasting relationship because our perspectives are so different.

I think the book *The 5 Love Languages* is a wonderful, helpful book with a lot of meaningful information. We have both read it and talked about how important it is to know your partner's love language and to honor it.

Sometimes I lose sight of the fact that one of "Sparkles" love languages is receiving little gifts. I think, "Well, it was just her birthday and I bought her a nice gift. We went out to dinner and had a great time and just returned from a fabulous two week cruise. What about all the ways I show her how much I love her every day?" From my perspective, everything is going along great and I'm thinking she's feeling loved and happy because *I know I am*!

I was surprised and felt defensive, at first, when she reminded me about her love language and that I hadn't sent her a card or brought her flowers in a long time. Then I thought, "What fertile ground this is for my *ego!*" My ego would have responded this way if I allowed it to. "What is the matter with you, we've done all these things together and have this terrific relationship and you are still not happy? There seems to always be something more that you want from me. Are you ever going to be satisfied? Always about you, boy are you selfish."

Instead of letting my ego run the show, I realized that Pat is grateful and appreciates all the gifts and things I do for her every day. She is constantly telling me how much she appreciates me and how happy she is with our relationship. I have to remember that one of her love languages is receiving small gifts and that it is meaningful and important to her. My pride and ego didn't like to admit that I had neglected her love language, but I had. I forget sometimes because it's not my love language and not so important to me. Just because it wasn't important to me, does not make it O.K. for me to neglect hers. Pat has suggested I write something on the calendar to help remind me each month.

I'm glad Pat made herself vulnerable by asking for what she needed and that she had the courage to bring things like this to the light, so they can be resolved. I want to love her the best way I can. It's important that we both are honest with one another about what we need in our relationship. It's the little things that will build up and become big problems if we don't deal with them.

I experience the energy and light of Love when I realize that ego is leading me to respond to a situation in an unloving manner. These experiences show me that Love is always present and active in my life guiding, providing, and protecting me.

JOURNAL

Do I believe my needs are less important than others?

Do I have a hard time asking for help?

What love language seems to be best for you? For the person closest to you?

Do I expect people to read my mind?

Chapter 12

Acceptance

*"Go with the flow. Force nothing.
Let it happen. . . trusting that whichever way it goes, it's for the best."*
~ *Mandy Hale*

Larry:

I have been reading Michael Singer's book, *The Surrender Experiment* and Eckhart Tolle's, *Stillness Speaks*. In both books, the authors encourage their readers to learn to accept whatever comes into their lives and not resist.

My understanding of what they're saying is that there is a Higher Power available to us and we can be helped by this Higher Power with any of our life's situations if we just remain open to that possibility. The experience may not be pleasant and may even be painful. We are encouraged to just accept, no matter what it is. If we feel that we can't accept what's happening, then accept that we can't accept it. By accepting, we stay open and we allow the Higher Power to grant us the gift that each life experience is bringing us. By resisting what's happening, we close ourselves to our Higher Power, which prevents us from receiving help.

For example: as I write this, I am being distracted by my neighbors' landscaper, who is using his loud leaf blower and weed whacker on one side of our home, and on the other side, they are doing construction. I can imagine my Higher Power observing me with a smile as I try to concentrate and accept this present life situation.

Accepting is becoming a new way of life for me. The other day, I decided to take a nap in the early afternoon. We don't have air conditioning, so we keep our windows and doors open. As I lay there, I became conscious of just how noisy it was outside. Dogs barking, people mowing lawns, hundreds of birds singing and chirping, etc. Usually, I would feel frustrated, impatient, angry, and get all stirred up and would go into the "poor me, poor me" mode.

I have been working very hard to learn to be more accepting and just allow things to be the way they are. I decided to accept everything that was going on outside and stay open to possibilities. Before I knew it, I was able to visualize this commotion outside as a large philharmonic orchestra playing a beautiful symphony. I know this sounds crazy, but it was really cool and before I knew it, I was asleep.

I know this is a small example of accepting, but if I can develop a new habit of staying open to life situations, I will be more open to accepting larger situations, as they arise.

I'm finding that it is easier to "accept life situations" when I live in the moment and don't pay attention to what may happen in the future or what has happened in the past. Tolle suggests that what is happening in a life situation is not us; we are "who is observing the situation." We are the one who is conscious of what is happening. When I remember that I am an observer in the experience, I stay open and accept what is happening at the moment.

It's such a positive experience to allow myself the opportunity to be flexible, to not be afraid of change, to be open to new ideas, and to accept the gift of joy and peace that is being offered to me. I send you love and light energy to assist you on your journey.

Acceptance

Pat:

I like to practice going with the flow and accepting "what is". It's not easy to go with the flow when there is a change in our lives, and we aren't happy about it. When I'm struggling and in pain, it's sometimes difficult to understand what's going on when I feel alone, as though Love has abandoned me. Are you able to go with the flow when something changes in your life or do you resist and feel frustrated and angry when things don't go your way? Of course, it depends on what the change is and whether it is something that you initiated and wanted.

Change is inevitable; sometimes painful and sometimes exhilarating. We are always evolving and so are the people we love. I have learned that all I can change is myself. It's not my job or responsibility to fix or try to change anyone else. It is my belief that everyone is doing the best they can, including myself.

Every day we experience change or loss; our bodies change, our emotions change, relationships change and our perspectives can change. We may experience an unexpected death of a loved one, a health crisis, divorce, a loss of job or home.

I believe change is good, although sometimes painful and hard. Do I always like to change? *No.* Do I sometimes complain and resist change? *Yes.* When I resist change, I may feel angry and frustrated and try to control the outcome. It is because I'm attached to what I want and think I know what's best for my life. That never works and I dig a hole for myself and cause more suffering. A Buddhist principle states that pain is inevitable, suffering is optional. We cause suffering when we don't allow ourselves to feel our feelings and pain.

When I *accept* change, I feel peaceful, relaxed, and free. It is like I am saying to the Universe, "I trust that whatever is happening is for my highest good, thank you God." When I'm open to change, I am saying *yes* to life and all the opportunities and experiences available to me, even though I may not see them. Acceptance is the answer to all of my problems. When I cannot accept every person, place, or thing as exactly as it is, I will not have peace.

Sometimes it takes time to accept changes in my life and I must allow myself, however long it takes, to feel and process my feelings. I must be patient, compassionate, and loving toward myself. For many years, I pushed my feelings down, especially anger. I wasn't encouraged or taught to feel and value my feelings. Shutting our emotions down makes us emotionally, spiritually, and physically sick. Today I know that feelings are a gift from God and to feel is to heal.

I no longer do a "spiritual bypass" (when we endeavor to use spirituality to cover our feelings) anymore and pretend that I'm fine when I'm not. I did that for many years putting on a happy face while inside I was dying and often didn't even know it. I didn't trust myself or others enough to be honest and real. Deep down, I was afraid that they wouldn't love me if I shared what I was experiencing.

It often takes time to move through the grief process and experience all of our feelings when we lose someone or something in our lives.

I know that acceptance is always the answer; but in order to get there, I must allow myself time to go through the grief process which may include feelings of denial, sadness, disappointment, anger, or depression. I have learned that feelings are not right or wrong and to give myself permission to feel whatever I'm feeling for as long as I need to and not push myself to go faster. It may take a day or a month or a year to work through something. During the grief process, it is important to love and be compassionate with myself, knowing that everything I need is inside of me.

Acceptance doesn't mean being a doormat. If someone is treating me poorly, I don't need to accept unacceptable behavior. For example: I can speak to the person, accept the situation, or I can leave.

Are you able to love yourself and give yourself what you need when things around you have changed and you are feeling sad or depressed?

I encourage you to trust yourself, Love, and the process and to know you are loved and that whatever is happening is for your highest good and that you are loved.

JOURNAL

Am I able to go with the flow or do I resist "what is"?

What are my losses that have been difficult to accept?

Have I done a "spiritual bypass" to avoid my feelings?

Chapter 13

Appreciation

"Make people feel welcomed, needed, and appreciated.
The greatest hunger people have is to be needed, wanted and loved."
~ Linda Andrade Wheeler

Larry:

Eckhart Tolle talks about how all of nature is alive and connected, everything and everyone is all part of one consciousness. He also suggests that nature doesn't realize how beautiful it is and how much it contributes to our joy and happiness until we communicate with it.

I thought that was an interesting observation. I had never realized that nature wouldn't automatically know the effect it had on the whole. It appears that the sky, sun, mountains, oceans, trees, flowers, and birds and all of nature need our recognition to understand that they are awesome, appreciated, and beautiful. They need to know that we are awestruck by their vastness and beauty, that just being near them and experiencing their fragrance and color fill our spirits and hearts with joy and happiness.

We live on Maui, one of the most beautiful places on earth. How often do we rush around all day, pass by all this natural beauty, and not recognize it? Doing this is such a disservice to us and nature. How much joy, happiness, and Love energy can we receive from just noticing the beauty of a flower? What about the incredibly beautiful sunsets we experience daily on Maui? They don't know how beautiful they are until we tell them how much joy and happiness we experience every time they appear.

I walk three miles most mornings just before the sun breaks over the mountains. Everything seems fresh and new, nature waking up to a great new day. The birds chatter deliriously at the prospect of a new day and adventure. I try to take everything in; telling the flowers they are beautiful and fill my heart with joy and gratitude.

Have you ever wondered how many people we meet each day or walk by, who may need just a little recognition and appreciation? My daily walks used to take me through one of our beautiful parks. Most days, I would see the same homeless person sitting on the grass near the walkway. I would greet him and sometimes stop and chat with him. One day, I commented, "You have found a great place to sit near the ocean."

He smiled and said, "Yes, I like it here. A lot of people walk by and some even say hi or good morning." It made me realize how important it is for all of us to be recognized and appreciated.

How often do we express our love and appreciation to our family members? For example, we may get caught up in the daily grind of making a living, providing for our family, raising children, etc. Some parents may think, "Hey, how about a little recognition and appreciation for all we do around here?" Some children may think, "We work hard in school to get good grades and be good students. We could use a little recognition and appreciation also." A few moments of love and appreciation can go a long way.

Pat and I realize how important it is to recognize and appreciate each other. Mostly in little ways like; thanking each other when we do a chore without having to be asked, making the bed, washing the dishes, or making lunch or dinner. Simple recognition and thank you goes a long way!

We appreciate one another when we show interest in each other's day and really listen and be present when one of us is sharing about something that is important to them. We communicate our love for one another when you would least expect it throughout the day. We say things like, "I love you; you have beautiful blue eyes, you look beautiful tonight" or a simple touch, hug, kiss or a shoulder rub is so valuable. A moment is never wasted when you give someone an expression of love.

What if we changed our attitude from one who needs to be served to one who will look for ways to be a vessel of Love and serve? Do you ever think of saying good morning or hi or aloha to someone you don't know? It may be the only time that day the person will be recognized and appreciated as an individual.

I have made it my practice to recognize and greet every person I meet. I think it is an important way to be a vessel of Love. Some return my greeting, and some do not, no worries. I have offered them the gift of Love and they can either accept it or refuse it. Not my problem. My responsibility is to offer the gift, with no strings attached.

When Pat lets me know how much she appreciates me, I feel valued and loved. It fills my love tank. There was a time in my life that I wasn't able to receive from others because I didn't feel worthy enough to receive. I encourage everyone to find little ways to recognize and appreciate each other. I think when we do that, we give the energy and light of Love a chance to manifest in all our lives.

Appreciation

Pat:

It is my desire to live my life to the fullest and *be* the woman God created me to be, using my gifts for the good of all. I choose to be a vessel of Love, have fun, play, and enjoy my life. I am not promised tomorrow, all I have is *now* and it's never too late to begin. I am worth it and deserve peace and love in my life.

We all want to be seen, heard, appreciated, and loved. Would you agree? It feels good when someone really listens and hears me, without trying to fix, control, give advice, or change me. They listen with their heart, rather than with their head and it feels different. It feels good when someone takes the time to see who I truly am and what I'm experiencing. If you have someone in your life who sees, hears, appreciates, and loves you, be grateful for you are blessed.

Whenever Larry goes to the market, a restaurant, or to the bank and the person is wearing a name tag, he always greets them using their name. It's a way of seeing someone and appreciating them, even or especially when doing a service job. It's such a small act of love and kindness, but it goes a long way and sometimes makes the person feel valued and recognized. I practice this now also and it feels good.

When Larry and I go to a restaurant, we often converse with the wait staff and somehow the conversation leads to the importance of gratitude and the power of Love in our lives. We often leave hugging one another.

Gladys was our waitress at Café Ole when we went for breakfast on Sunday. I complimented her on her beautiful smile. I often compliment others when I see something I like; something they are wearing or their beautiful eyes or their smile. This is my way of showing kindness and appreciating what I see in others.

I keep small inspirational cards with me in my purse. When Spirit leads me, I give a card to someone or leave one at the table when I leave for the next person to find. I was led to randomly pick one for Gladys. It was *believe in yourself, and you will be unstoppable.*

When I handed it to her, her whole face lit up and she said, "Thank you, I really needed this today. I'm going to put this where I can see it every day. This will really help me, and you made my day. I'm just getting into real estate and I'm struggling with not feeling good enough." Of course, we were all smiling and hugged one another when we left the restaurant.

I have a daily "appreciation practice" that I have been doing for many years. Right before going to sleep, I review the day in my mind and think about all the things I appreciate about myself. For example, I ate healthily, I called a friend to say hello, I was patient with the clerk at the store. It really feels good to recognize my gifts and growth.

JOURNAL

Do I take the time to appreciate the beauty around me?

Do I recognize and appreciate myself?

Do I feel seen, heard, and appreciated?

Chapter 14

Celebrating Our Growth

"Just try to be the best you can be;
never cease trying to be the best you can be.
That's in your power."
~ John Wooden

Pat:

I'm celebrating my growth and the courage to "go within" for my answers. I am committed to my spiritual journey and allowing whatever needs to come up to be transformed. I no longer medicate my feelings but allow myself to feel everything. I know that to feel is to heal and feelings are a gift from God.

I confronted Larry about a comment he made that seemed inappropriate the night before when we had company. He listened but didn't have the same perspective that I had. In fact, it was just the opposite. The good news is that I didn't argue with him, try to control him and get him to see it my way. I trusted my perception and feelings and didn't have to make Larry wrong and me right. This is definitely growth.

I knew what happened wasn't resolved yet and we needed some time apart before discussing it further. I spent time alone in prayer, writing, and asking Spirit for guidance and clarity. I have learned the importance of loving myself first and filling up my tank before I can genuinely love another.

In past relationships, it may have taken me a week or a month or a year to share my feelings. Because I was afraid to share my feelings, resentment would build up and it would often come out sideways. I would minimize or deny things that happened because I didn't want to rock the boat. There were times that I didn't even know what I was feeling and would ask friends, "Would you feel this way if this happened to you?"

The growth for me is that I trusted myself, my feelings, Larry, and the strength of our relationship to be honest and share my perception, even though it was different from his.

As I prayed about it, this is what was revealed to me.

I'm responsible for:

- Myself, my perceptions, and my feelings.
- Giving myself the attention and time that I need when I need it.
- To set boundaries about what I will and won't do.
- To change what I can change.
- To follow my heart, trust myself and change my mind when I want to.
- To communicate what I want and don't want.

When I returned home, I shared with Larry all that I learned. I was clear, straightforward forward, and non-judgmental. We had a great conversation and I felt loved and heard.

Here is another experience where I was able to see my growth.

We were already late for the dance on Saturday night when I realized that I forgot my dancing shoes. We were halfway there, and I couldn't dance in the shoes I was wearing. When I looked on the floor and saw that my shoes weren't there, I said to Larry, "I forgot my shoes."

Without any apparent upset or judgment, he said, "We will turn around as soon as I can find an opening."

I said calmly, "I know there is a reason."

The good news for me is that I recognized immediately that I didn't beat up on myself at all. I shared with Larry that in the past, I would have done a job on myself. I was led to "act" out what I would have done to myself in the past. I asked Larry to play along with me as if it was really true because I wanted to feel the difference in how we actually handled it and what I would have felt if I had retreated back to old behaviors of beating up on myself.

With frustration and anger, I said, "Oh sh—I forgot my shoes. I can't believe that I did that. What is wrong with me? I never forget my shoes. What a dummy I am." Larry "acted as if" he was angry at me for my stupidity and went along with me for a few minutes. When we were done, I was shocked at the difference I felt. My heart was pounding, and I was now angry at him as well as myself. This could have erupted into a big fight and we wouldn't have made it to the dance.

Instead, we were both peaceful and drove calmly home to get my shoes. I have been practicing for a long time trusting that all is well, that everything happens for a reason, and everything is in perfect and divine order. It just felt so natural to trust. I don't know if this will happen every time. I sure do hope so because the ending felt so much better. We arrived one hour late to the dance and had a wonderful time.

Celebrating Our Growth

Larry:

Pat and I were discussing how we had grown and changed. I think I have made progress in some areas and none in others. I've grown in patience and living in the moment.

I grew up believing that the man of the household had the responsibility to make sure everyone was happy. When there was a problem, I thought it was my job to fix it or offer a solution. I realize that my perspectives about relationships came from this belief and my behaviors reflected this.

Pat has helped me to understand that when she shares something that is troubling her, she is not expecting me to fix it. She needs to share it and wants me to just listen. After I have listened, I ask her, "Is there anything you would like me to do to support you?"

The area I've grown most in is allowing Pat to share her feelings without offering an answer or solution. When I'm able to do this, it really feels good because I don't have the pressure to make it right or solve the problem. It's no longer my responsibility and it's a great weight off my shoulder. I wish I had known this a long time ago. I'm learning that I can still love Pat and be there for her without trying to fix what's bothering her. She is an intelligent woman who can handle her own challenges.

I really want my default to be "I choose Love" in all situations and with all people instead of blaming, judging, shaming, copping an attitude, or feeling resentful when things don't go my way or the way I think they should. Can you relate?

It takes lots of practice to have my default be "I choose Love". It doesn't come naturally to choose Love when I'm pissed or think I've been wronged or not respected. My natural tendency is to shut down or want to "get back" and judge the other person when I'm hurt or angry.

Spirit always gives me the perfect opportunities to practice choosing Love. Sometimes it may take me a while but when I'm conscious, I see everything as opportunities to grow and change. For example: when Pat forgot her dancing shoes and we had to turn around and come all the way home, I remained calm, patient, and open to the energy of Love. In the past I would have allowed ego to bring me to the place of judgment and blame and contributed negative energy to the whole situation.

We all have expectations of what we hope for or want things to look like. It's probably impossible not to have expectations. We go on vacation and we expect or hope the weather will be beautiful. We have a date with a new person and hope it will go well. Of course, being positive is healthy and there is nothing wrong with that.

When things don't go my way, I have the opportunity to accept "what is" and live in the moment. When I accept things or people just as they are, I have peace. I lose my peace and serenity when I want to control people and how they do things or don't do things.

I have learned that I am responsible for myself and my reactions, feelings, and behaviors. We fail to understand that all we have control over is ourselves. I cannot control anyone else to do something the way I expect them to do it.

For example, I was expecting an event to go in a certain direction with a friend. I had it pictured in my mind how I wanted it to unfold. When it didn't go the way I pictured it, I felt resentful, at first, and judged my friend. I allowed myself to feel my disappointment because I didn't want to do a "spiritual bypass" and push my feelings down. A spiritual bypass is when we don't allow ourselves to feel our feelings, especially anger, disappointment, frustration, and grief.

Instead of wallowing in resentment and disappointment, I started to repeat to myself, "I choose Love, I choose Love." Within a few minutes, I felt peaceful and the resentment was gone. I have heard that "An expectation is a premeditated resentment."

When I saw my friend the next day, by choosing Love, I didn't feel any resentment or judgment and we had a great day together. The outcome would have been very different, and I would have missed out on a great spiritual experience if I hadn't chosen Love.

I am grateful that I recognize my behaviors and that I have the tools to change myself one day at a time. I am learning not to take things personally, to detach from outcomes, and to know that I am not responsible for another person's happiness.

JOURNAL

Am I able to confront my partner when I'm upset?

Where have I grown in my relationships with others?

Am I afraid to be honest and share my feelings?

Chapter 15

Choices

*"I believe we are solely responsible for our choices,
and we have to accept the consequences of every deed, word,
and thought throughout our lifetime."*
~ Elisabeth Kubler-Ross

Larry:

I believe Love is a gift waiting to be accepted. I have a choice to say yes or no. I think making the decision to accept the gift of Love is at first a head thing and when I say yes, then it becomes a matter of the heart when I must make myself vulnerable and open. Sometimes, that involves risk! In a love relationship, one could think, "Will it last, will I get hurt, can I trust love?" I am much better at accepting and loving myself than I ever have been before. Since I've accepted the gift of Love in my life, I'm more able to Love myself and be the vessel of Love that God intended me to be.

I asked Pat this question, "How do we maintain our relationship with ourselves when we are in a love relationship with another person?" For many years, I ignored my relationship with myself and gave it all to the person I was in a relationship with. When the relation-ship was over, I didn't have anything left to support me.

A healthy relationship will allow each person to have a life apart from the other, friends, interests, hobbies, etc. When we have developed a relationship with ourselves, we most likely will want to spend some time alone. It isn't that we don't love the other person or don't want to be with them. I like my own company and value that time alone. I walk three miles every day and when I'm driving my car, I don't use the radio because I value that time alone. If the relationship is secure and there is trust, we would encourage and support our partners to develop a relationship with themselves.

My experience with failed relationships has taught me that it requires a lot of work, especially on my part. I am continuously finding opportunities to change, grow, and learn and not to *resist what is*.

Life and relationships are about *choices*:

- How do I know which choice will be best?
- Will the choice I make be better for me or for my partner?
- Will the choice I make be better for our relationship?
- Am I being selfish if I make the choice that is best for me?
- Am I being true to myself with the choice I am making?

Perhaps it's time to realize that loving one another reminds us that we are all connected. The one common thread that connects us is the energy and light of Love. Yes, we are all different in some ways and sometimes we say and do things that hurt each other. We are not perfect. I don't believe perfection is what it's all about. Love will show us how to forgive, heal, and move on. I believe life's purpose is to learn how to love ourselves so we can become vessels of Love. I invite you on this journey and together we can overcome our differences and walk this journey of Love together.

Alan Cohen writes in his book, *Wisdom of the Heart*:

> "It isn't selfish to love yourself. It is the first step to true kindness. Only when you love who and what you are can you love others in the way that they yearn to be cared for. Very few people err by loving themselves too much; most err by loving themselves too little."

We will always be given opportunities to make loving choices. For example, while working in the kitchen, I like everything to be in order and I clean as I go. Pat has a different perspective and order is not that important to her. When she is cooking, she has no problem with spreading out all over the counters. I have a choice whether to become frustrated, angry, and judgmental or I can allow her to be who she is. I can choose to accept the situation with patience and love.

Choices

Pat:

We all have times in our lives when everything just seems to work out and there are no stressors and we just go sailing along our merry way. We are on top of the world, peaceful and our prayers are being answered, and we experience daily miracles. I love these times and I want them to last forever.

Then there are times when it feels like everything is happening at once and we feel stressed and out of sorts. We have lost our peace. We may be struggling with health challenges, finances, or family/relationship problems. It's one problem after another and we feel like we just can't handle another problem.

What are you experiencing today? Are you peaceful and things are "easy breezy" or are you stressed and want to give up and throw in the towel and say enough is enough?

When we are feeling stressed and feel like we are sinking, we can make the *choice* to either trust Love or fear. By choosing Love, we allow Love's power to guide us and show us the way. A moment is never wasted when you give someone an expression of love

We are invited to practice gratitude when we don't feel like it or when we are struggling and want to give up. I used to think I was being tested when I experienced challenges. I don't think it's a test anymore, but rather an opportunity to learn to *trust* and surrender to Spirit more deeply. Gratitude is usually the last thing we want to do when we are suffering, right?

I have given Spirit control of my life, which means Spirit is driving my car and I have *chosen* to be in the back seat. This doesn't mean that I don't make decisions or am inactive. Quite the opposite. I am moving forward in my life and going within and asking Spirit for guidance with every decision I make. I know there is no right or wrong or good or bad decision. It is my belief that everything happens for a reason and for my highest good.

When I *choose* to give up the controls to God, I am peaceful, safe, relaxed, knowing all is in the perfect and right order. I accept "what is" even though I might not like it. I trust Love is working in the background, especially when I don't see what's happening or what the gift is.

I am *choosing* to turn up the dial of my *gratitude attitude*, instead of complaining, obsessing, and worrying. I have a few stressors in my life that I am dealing with today, but I am affirming and practicing, "Everything is flowing with peace, ease, and grace."

For example, I'm selling my condo in Rhode Island. I was told that it is a seller's market and I would have no problem selling it because there was a shortage of homes in the area. This is stressful living 5,000 miles away and not being there. The first cash offer fell through within a few days of the offer. When my son called this week and said, "We have an offer on the condo." I was thrilled and relieved. The offer was incredibly low, especially after we had already reduced the price by 20,000 dollars.

After talking it over with the real estate broker and my son, we decided I would be giving it away and the right buyer had just not shown up yet. She suggested when they move out we make some improvements, which would help the sale of the house.

I am coming to Rhode Island for our annual family reunion and will be able to do the work with the help of my children, grandchildren, and hired professionals to paint and do a deep cleaning in the condo.

This is not what I *planned* to do on my visit with my family, but it is what is presenting itself and I am *choosing* to accept "what is" and stay in gratitude. Even though this is stressful and not what I planned to do on our family vacation, I am trusting that Love's light and energy will sustain me through this experience. It truly was a labor of love working together with my family to make the improvements. We had fun and laughed a lot.

JOURNAL

Have I made the choice to accept the gift of Love in my life?

How do I maintain a relationship with myself when I am in a relation-ship?

Have I chosen to give Spirit control of my life?

Chapter 16

Communication

"Communication to a relationship is like oxygen to life.
Without it, it dies."
~ Tony Gaskins

Pat:

I love to celebrate milestones, birthdays, anniversaries, and holidays. I looked forward to celebrating our two year anniversary of being together. Larry and I talked about going out to lunch and doing some-thing special, but nothing had been planned yet.

We were having our morning time together when the subject of how we were going to celebrate our anniversary came up. Larry turned to me and said, "You're not expecting a gift, are you?" I was taken off guard because I hadn't thought about it and automatically said, "Oh no." By now you know my number one love language is gifts and cards. We finished our time together and got ready for the day. Some-thing didn't feel right inside.

"Why did I say no to an anniversary gift when gifts are my love language?"

I thought about an incident that happened with Larry a few weeks ago when I asked him the question, "Would you like me to pay for the dance we are going to tonight?"

He said, "No, but it would feel better if you wanted to pay for something to just say, 'I would like to treat you tonight.'" I understood what he meant and agreed to do that.

At first, I wasn't going to say anything to Larry about his remark about not expecting a gift, but it felt like an "ouch" and similar to when I asked him if he wanted me to pay for the dance. I decided to bring it up to him and share my feelings. I could feel myself tearing up as we began to talk, and I felt childish.

As we talked, I became aware that my emotional upset and tears were not about what was happening today but was about my past and being forgotten on anniversaries and birthdays in my marriage. I was surprised because that happened almost fifty years ago, and I have done the inner work of forgiveness and letting go. I know that everything that has ever happened to us is still in our bodies and the original wound can be triggered by a present event.

Larry explained to me what he meant by his remark. He said, "It wasn't that I didn't want to buy you a gift, it was just that I didn't know if you expected a gift because celebrating anniversaries was not something that was important to me."

It is my belief that we are in relationships to heal one another. Even though I felt very vulnerable, I found myself in his loving embrace and allowed myself to cry and be healed by his love. What was significant for me is that he *heard* me and was willing to love me how I wanted and needed to be loved. Even though it wasn't important to celebrate the way I did, he was willing to do it for me. That alone was a huge healing.

As I sat to reflect on what happened, I felt some shame and guilt about my love language being gifts. I love giving and receiving gifts. I needed to love and appreciate myself and my love language, instead of feeling shame and guilt.

As we finished our discussion Larry said, "I am the bad guy."

With tears running down my cheeks I said, "Oh my God, you didn't hear me. *You are the good guy*. It is your love that is healing deep wounds from my past." I assured him how loved and cared for I felt.

Later during the day, Larry said, "I know what I can get you for our anniversary. I will buy your new dance shoes if you would like."

I smiled and said, "I would love that." It will be the perfect gift since we both love to dance. I ordered the shoes and I will be dancing my little feet off in a few days.

Because we strive to live in Love consciousness and not allow our egos to run the show, we were able to be fearlessly honest and vulnerable with ourselves and each other. Instead of the situation escalating, it was resolved in a loving, peaceful manner.

None of this would have happened if I had not communicated to Larry my feelings. We grow closer to one another every time we are willing to share our vulnerable feelings without judgment or resentment.

Communication

Larry:

I think the experience of gift giving that Pat shares shows how different our perspectives can be and why it's important to be able to communicate and discuss it in a rational, loving manner.

Celebrating holidays, birthdays, anniversaries, and special days are not high on my list of priorities. I tend to just let them go by and sometimes not even notice them. I am grateful for the life I have and welcome every day as a "special" gift. I know that Pat's number one love language is cards and gifts.

The other day when I asked her, "Are you expecting a gift?" What I meant was, "Is this a gift giving occasion or will a card and lunch be OK?" Her perspective of what I said was different than my perspective. We could have wasted time and energy contesting that issue. Instead, we chose to listen to each other's perspectives in an honest, supportive, and loving way. I didn't criticize or belittle her. I understood her feelings because I know her history. I felt like I had let her down by not remembering how important her number one love language was to her. Pat didn't make me feel like the bad guy. Instead, she communicated that my support and caring love helped her to heal.

Relationships are not easy; we have to give them plenty of attention. There are always opportunities to heal and grow. They're like planting a garden, one has to constantly water and weed if you want it to be successful.

We need to love ourselves enough to speak up when something is bothering us and not sweep it under the rug. If we are not honest and push it down, it will come out sideways down the road. It is difficult to bring up an unpleasant subject and we have to put our ego aside to discuss it in a loving and caring way. It's important to understand that our partner may have a different understanding or perspective of the situation and it isn't a question of who's right and who's wrong, it is just that we are different.

I endeavor to be patient, kind, and open, allowing the light of Love to show me the way. Pat and I will continue our journey together in gratitude, for the gift we are to each other.

JOURNAL

Do I speak up and express my needs?

Do I sweep things under the rug to maintain peace?

Do I give the silent treatment to my partner when I'm upset?

Chapter 17

Compatibility

"A lasting relationship isn't about marriage.
It's about compatibility and communication.
And you both need to want it to work."
~ Goldie Hawn

Pat:

I recently looked up the definition of compatibility. It is the "ability to exist and perform in harmonious or agreeable combination."

I have never been in a relationship that is more compatible than I am with Larry. We always comment to one another how well we get along. We not only love one another, but we like each other, support each other's journey, enjoy each other's company, laugh at each other's silly jokes, and find it easy to talk to one another. Larry can make me laugh and we laugh a lot.

We respect each other's opinions, even when we disagree about something. We cherish each other for who we are and give each other the freedom to be ourselves. We strive to be authentic with one another and share our feelings openly and honestly. We listen to one another and communicate well.

Compatibility is much more than just getting along with your partner. It is knowing that your partner has compatible moral values and opinions on the most important issues in your life. Larry and I complement each other spiritually, intellectually, physically, and emotionally. We each have our own interests, as well as similar interests that we do together. Our temperaments are similar in that we both like relaxing, naps, going for rides, going out to lunch, and just being together.

Something came up for us this week that we were able to communicate about and work through because of our willingness, to be honest, and share what is important to us. This was the first Christmas I wouldn't be spending time with my children. It is important that Larry and I start new traditions for Christmas.

I suggested to Larry that on Christmas day we invite some of our friends to our home who don't have family here for a potluck. He seemed agreeable and we started to invite our friends. Everyone was happy to be invited and to share it with us.

I felt surprised when Larry shared his feelings with me this week because they were not compatible with mine. We both had different "needs and wants" for Christmas day. He was clearly not excited about having people over like I was. It wasn't that he didn't like the people we invited over, he really did. He shared how stressful it is because of his past experiences of being in the catering business. He told me, "I am agreeable to do this because I love you and know it is important to you, especially your first Christmas away from your family."

I was quiet and listened to his feelings and tried to be as understanding as I could be. Although I was grateful for his honesty in sharing his thoughts and feelings with me, I felt disappointed and wondered what the best thing to do would be for both of us. I didn't want him to be stressed that we were having a party and I wanted to support him and his needs. I also wanted to support me and my needs to have friends over.

I sensed this was an opportunity for me to grow and to let go of old codependent behaviors and beliefs. For so many years, I felt responsible for my loved one's behaviors and feelings and thought their behavior was a reflection on me.

I know I am not responsible for Larry's feelings and behaviors and I don't have to fix or change him. I am responsible for my own behaviors and feelings and keeping my vibration high. I choose to live in peace and joy by practicing detachment with love. I prayed and asked God for help in how to handle this situation.

At first, I thought the best thing to do would be to say nothing to Larry and just move forward with the plans. I didn't want to escalate it or make it worse for him. I then decided to ask him, "How can I help you get what you want, and your needs met and feel less stressed?"

Compatibility

Larry:

It looks like I have a "challenge" and an "opportunity" to grow at the same time when it comes to socializing and partying. I find this very stressful because of my past history of being in the food industry for thirty-two years (sixteen year's operating my own catering business and sixteen years as a manager of an industrial cafeteria.) Planning and providing food for clients' special occasions was a stressful and demanding career. In the catering business, you are judged by how satisfied your customers are with their events. As the owner of the business, I felt responsible and strived to have everything perfect. It was a reflection on me if something went wrong.

When I retired, I promised myself that thirty-two years of this kind of stress was enough and that I would not allow myself to experience stressful situations like this again. For fourteen years, I have been successful at doing this until now.

I think Pat and I are very compatible, and this situation offers us an opportunity to be flexible, loving, and understanding with each other. I know that we will figure it out and both benefit from this experience.

This is Pat's first time away from family during the Christmas holidays and I wanted to be as supportive as possible. She has a desire to have a party on Christmas day and I would have been happy to take in a movie and dinner or take everybody out to a restaurant.

When Pat suggested, "Let's have a party" my stress button automatically kicked in because I didn't want to feel that kind of pressure again and put myself in a situation where my actions could be judged as successful or failure.

For most of my life, I would be all right with just going along with what someone else wanted because it wasn't worth the hassle for me to complain. I may not have even known what I wanted. Now as I'm learning to love myself and become more conscious, when I don't want to do something and I am not happy with a situation, I bring it up for discussion.

Although I wanted to support Pat and not disappoint her, I decided to be honest and shared my feelings with her. I thought perhaps she didn't understand the magnitude of the stress I experienced all those years in my profession. I felt frustrated and fearful because I didn't want to be put in that vulnerable position of the possibility of failure again. Yet, I had agreed to have a party for Christmas as a sign of my love for Pat and to be willing to face and heal my past.

When Pat asked me, "How can I help you get what you want and your needs met and feel less stressed," I didn't even have an answer for her. We discussed my feeling "responsible" for everything and having to do things perfectly. I acknowledged that if I changed the belief that I have to do everything perfectly, I would feel less stressed.

Pat and I agreed that she would "shoulder" all the stress by planning and purchasing all the supplies, food, and drinks. Sounds like a good plan for me because after all, it was her idea. I am confident that we will work this out because Love conquers all. We will work together one moment at a time and the Christmas party will be fine.

Pat followed through with all of the plans, which enabled me not to feel stressed out. By being honest and sharing with one another what was important for us, we were able to celebrate and have a great day with our friends.

Whichever way you are celebrating the holidays, regardless of how you picture God welcome everyone with Love, forgive everyone with love and open your hearts to the greatest gift possible, *the gift of Love.*

JOURNAL

Am I in a relationship at present that is compatible?

Do I feel responsible for my partner's behavior and see it as a reflection of me?

Am I a perfectionist and want to do things perfectly?

Chapter 18

Disagreements

"How different we are, you and I so much alike, together complete."
~ Linda Andrade Wheeler

Larry:

We are human, and just like every other couple, we have disagreements or get upset with one another. They don't become a threat to our relationship by becoming a blown out of proportion, drama filled challenge because of the way we have learned to handle them. First and foremost, we respect one another and during disagreements, we don't forget that. We allow each other's perspective to be expressed and *heard*.

If the situation has caused one of us to become emotional, we give ourselves time to think about it before we discuss it. We try to stay flexible and endeavor to get to a place where we can resolve the issue without blaming and it becomes an I win and you lose situation.

We have discovered two words that have a healing effect on disagreements, they are "I'm sorry." We have developed a system when one of us says something to the other that hurts their feelings we say "ouch" that hurts, which gives the person an opportunity to explain or apologize.

We understand that at this stage in life, we don't have a lot of circumstances that can cause stress and challenges like a younger couple may have. For example: raising and providing for children, stressful jobs, buying a home, making decisions for their future, etc.

We do have other issues that can cause stress in our lives, for example, the cost of health care, health issues, senior housing, what happens if we outlive our retirement funds, and how will I manage if I'm alone.

Although we have similar temperaments, likes, and values, we do have differences that we have managed to work through.

I read directions carefully and Pat doesn't. I prefer to stay home, and Pat is more social and enjoys going out. I don't go to the beach because I have skin cancer and Pat loves to walk the beach. I am more private about my life and Pat does a blog every week and shares her life experiences. I don't like to ask for help and Pat doesn't have a problem with it. I am a perfectionist and Pat is not. I go to bed later and Pat goes to bed early. I don't like the spotlight and Pat likes it. I like order in the kitchen and Pat is more of a free spirit. When I'm not feeling well, I prefer to be alone and when Pat's not feeling well, she wants me around.

I take my time with things and Pat tends to go fast. For example: One late afternoon, we were editing the book and Pat was becoming impatient and short with me. I was becoming frustrated and realized that to keep the peace, I said, "Let's finish this tomorrow."

It works for us because we have learned to give each other freedom and space to be who we are and accept our differences with patience and love. Differences are not bad because we learn from one another.

The key to not letting these issues become stressful is to live in the moment, one day at a time and not worry about the future, until it becomes the present. We understand that Love/God has been watching over us for a long time and we trust that this will not change. We have lived many years to get here; it is time to enjoy life and not allow ego to stress us out and take our peace away.

Disagreements

Pat:

As I thought about this topic, I have to admit Larry and I don't have many disagreements. We are both pretty "low key" and can usually talk things out and come to a peaceful resolution where we both feel our needs are met. We also both have a great sense of humor and humor will often dissipate an argument.

When I make a suggestion and Larry doesn't agree with it, instead of getting into an argument, I have learned to let it go and let him sit with it. It is hard to not control or push my ideas. Often, after he thinks about it, he changes his mind. If he doesn't change his mind, it wasn't meant to be, and I accept it.

Have you ever had the experience of "hovering" over a loved one or being "hovered over?" It could be an adult child, close friend, spouse, or parent. You find yourself too invested or involved in whatever they are doing or *not* doing. You think you are helping them and give them advice and tell them what to do both subtly and not so subtly. You may worry or obsess about them.

For me, "hovering" is about fear. I am afraid my loved one will suffer because of their behaviors and get hurt. When I focus and "hover" over a loved one, I lose my peace of mind. Whenever I try to control or fix another person because I think I know what's right for them, I lose my peace.

You may have heard the term helicopter mom. What about "helicopter wife or husband"? I was married to Larry for a short time when I found myself "hovering" over him. I was in trouble because I knew better. Old behaviors die hard. Luckily, I recognized it quickly and we discussed it and how it felt for both of us. I do not want to be, nor will I be a "helicopter wife"!

While we were driving in the car to the airport in Rhode Island with lots of cars going in and out of lanes, I was advising Larry how to drive. I burst out laughing when he turned to me and said, "Would you please land your helicopter?" It was absolutely perfect, and I got the message loud and clear. Since then, we have used the "helicopter concept" whenever we feel the other is "hovering". It is such a gentle way to communicate in a loving manner. We will continue to remind each other when either one of us needs to land our helicopter.

It's been several years, and we haven't needed to remind each other to land our helicopters until this week! Larry asked me to "land my helicopter" after I gave him my opinion about calling his doctor. He had been struggling with sinus problems for the past few weeks and it has been pretty intense. He tried over the counter allergy medicine, but it made it worse. He cannot breathe at night and has to sit in his chair to sleep. He may sleep for an hour and then wake up and have difficulty breathing again. Consequently, he is exhausted and takes cat naps during the day.

It was really scary for me watching him suffer and not being able to do anything about it. I didn't know if he would be alive in the morning or not. I felt upset about his unwillingness to call his doctor and get medical treatment. I thought he was being "stubborn" and no matter what I said, he wouldn't listen.

Larry is an adult and knows what he needs to do for his body. If he doesn't want to take a medication or see the doctor, that is up to him. I trust that he will figure it out and do what's best for him. I don't want to hover over his every move and tell him what to do. This is not respecting him by trying to convince him to do something he doesn't want to do. If I have given my opinion once, then I need to let it go and let God. I have learned to pray and send love. I asked Spirit to speak to Larry's heart. Although it takes a great deal of patience not to say anything, this always works. Here is what Spirit said:

> *"You must trust that I am in charge. Larry is trying to do this on his own and will realize when he needs to ask for help. Trust me and let go of fear. I am in charge. Choose Love."*

I knew Larry had a difficult night and wanted to ask him in the morning, "What are you going to do about it?" Instead, I said nothing and trusted God.

Larry looked at me and said, "I'm going to call the doctor today."

I said, "Thank you Jesus for answering my prayer." Larry called the doctor that day and was prescribed a medication and is feeling better.

There will always be challenges and disagreements in every relationship. What's important is that we respect and listen to each other's perspectives and not try to control or change the other person.

JOURNAL

Do I feel respected, acknowledged, and heard in my relationship?

Am I able to say I'm sorry or do I blame and hold a resentment?

Do I try to control and push to get my way?

Chapter 19

Ego

"There is only one of the two that can reside in our hearts GOD or ego.
If God is in ego is out."
~ A.R. Rahman

Pat:

Whenever I know the truth of who I am as a vessel of Love and a magnificent, beautiful, loving, light being, my ego acts up (and sometimes viciously) because it doesn't want me to know the truth of who I am. It wants me to believe that I am separate from Source and alone.

Spirit revealed to me how the "not good enough" belief still infiltrates my thoughts sometimes and brings me into fear. I believe it is a universal core belief that needs to come to the light to be released and healed because it is not *true*. It is insidious and shows up where I'm vulnerable and when I'm least expecting it. I was surprised when it "showed up" in my relationship with my husband, especially after feeling so loved.

Larry and I had a busy day and didn't spend much time sharing with one another, as we usually do. I woke up the next morning with a "fearful" uneasy feeling in my gut. I didn't know what it was until I sat and meditated, prayed, and journaled.

I felt fear that our relationship "wasn't good enough" because we hadn't spent much time together the day before. As I sat with it, I realized how absurd and crazy the "story" was that I had made up. I think this was an example of my ego trying to sabotage me and make me lose my peace.

The truth is I feel heard, seen, trusted, protected, supported, cared for, nurtured, accepted, understood, respected, and loved. *And that is more than enough.*

I share this story with you to help you recognize where your ego may be robbing you of your peace by telling you that you are not enough, you don't have enough, or you don't do enough.

My ego robbed me of my peace for as long as I can remember, probably forever. The only problem was that I didn't recognize it as my ego. It felt *real* and I believed it, even though I was successful in my career, written a book, and had a Master's degree. It was this nagging inner voice that constantly whispered in my ear, "You are not good enough and deserving or worthy of Love."

What I know today is that my ego voice is not real and is an illusion. All there is is Love and I am not separate from God. We are *one*. Nothing else matters and it is just part of the play and only a dream. I recently participated in a meditation and my ego showed up as a "boogie man" dressed in black. As I prayed and meditated, here is what came to me. The boogie man comes out at night and in dreams to scare me. When I "wake up" I realize it isn't real, but an illusion. Whenever I feel jealous, judge another, feel less than, compare myself, I recognize this as my ego that is not real and not *Love*.

This is a time of "Awakening" and we are all waking up from the dream of separation in our own way. Some of us are kicking and screaming and blaming others for our problems. We are invited to take responsibility for ourselves and to see the truth of who we are. We are Love, we were created in Love and Love is all there is.

Today, I recognize when my ego shows up to torment and scare me. I acknowledge it for what it is and say, you are not real, *I choose Love*. The ego knows exactly where I am sensitive and will attack in the area that I am most vulnerable to constantly rob me of my peace and serenity.

There are so many ways ego shows up and we have to be vigilant and call ego by its name. It loses its power when we identify it as ego as we bring it into the light and choose Love. Are you in the habit of constantly judging yourself after a conversation or gathering with friends? Do you say things like, "I talked too much or not enough? I should not have shared that, or I was to negative?"

Do you recognize that it is your ego, or do you believe it is true about yourself and then beat up on yourself?

Ego

Larry:

The ego is our "false self" and the current state of humanity. Ego shows up in our lives through our thoughts and its negative energy causes us a great deal of stress, pain, and suffering. Once we allow ourselves to be directed into the egoic state of mind, we find ourselves in a downward spiral towards a life of negativity and fear.

We believe we are not good enough, handsome or pretty enough, too thin or heavy, too tall or short, or not smart enough. Any negative thoughts you have are brought about by the ego. The ego will encourage you to be unkind and disrespectful, to judge others so you can feel better about yourself, and to see everyone else wrong and you right.

For example, we have a sliding screen door that leads to our lanai. It doesn't slide well, and I have tried to fix it, without much success. If it isn't closed just right, it stays open and leaves a space.

I asked Pat to be careful and make sure the door was closed all the way when she uses it. I am concerned that centipedes, cockroaches, mice, or rats will gain entry if the door is not closed all the way. It is not as much of a priority for Pat as it is for me. Although she has tried to close it tight when she goes outside, sometimes she doesn't think about it and there is a space open. I was bitten by a centipede a few years ago and it wasn't much fun. From my perspective, closing the door is particularly important and I would like to have it closed all the time. I know if critters get in, Pat is not going to dispatch them and will call me to do it. For Pat, it's not that important.

Wow, my ego had a ball with that; it tells me, "What the heck is wrong with her, why can't she close the door all the way? What is she five years old? Why is it a big deal to just close the door all the way?" My ego says, "She's wrong and I'm right." I can see how ego is trying to cause drama and negativity in our relationship if I allow it.

After several months of feeling frustrated every time, I looked at the opened door, it became obvious that the situation wasn't going to change. I could continue to feel frustrated or I could do something about it.

I finally asked myself, "How would a vessel of Love handle the situation?" This is what I learned. My options were:

- Talk to Pat about it. I did.
- I could move; I don't like that option.
- I could feel resentful every time I see the door opened.
- I could put on my big boy pants and take responsibility for the door.

Yea! I like the option of taking responsibility for the door, no one is right or wrong. When I see the door open now, I just close it. Love showed me my ego had been running the show. To be a vessel of Love requires me to look at myself and discover what needs to be changed. I changed my perspective and took the power away from ego. Taking responsibility for the situation certainly brought more peace and harmony in our lives.

Of course, this is just a small example of how ego will try to disrupt a relationship and cause separateness. If we are open and conscious of the power and energy of Love, it will become our default and will help us in all kinds of situations.

JOURNAL

Where has my ego robbed me of my peace?

Am I a helicopter wife or husband?

How does ego disrupt my relationships?

Chapter 20

Faith

"Faith in God includes faith in His timing."
~ *Anonymous*

Pat:

Larry and I were invited to a birthday party a few years ago while we were just friends. I had never been to the house before. When Larry and I walked out to the lanai overlooking the expansive 180 degree view of the ocean, I was blown away. I remember clearly looking at Larry and saying, "This is where I want to live."

A year later, I heard that my friend who lived in the beautiful house with the view was thinking about moving. I called him immediately and said, "Would you consider recommending me to the owner?"

"Yes, I will let you know when I decide if I'm going to move."

I really felt excited about the possibility of living in that house, even though it seemed financially impossible for me to do at the time. In the meantime, my landlord informed me that he would be renovating my ohana and I would have to move. I waited, prayed, and trusted in divine timing.

My friend finally contacted me and said, "I will be moving and am recommending you to the owner." Interestingly, the owner lived in Rhode Island, where I moved to Maui from. I contacted the owner and she was thrilled to have the high recommendation of a new prospective tenant. Another synchronicity of how God guides us and opens doors for our highest good.

Since I had to vacate my ohana before my dream house was available, I was "homeless" for six weeks. I put my furniture in storage and spent time with friends, who lovingly shared their homes with me. Six weeks later, I moved into my dream home overlooking the ocean and doubled my rent!

That was a *big* step in faith as I went from 1200 dollars a month to 2500 dollars a month. As I think about it, I know I followed my heart because my head said, "Are you crazy? Where are you going to get the extra money from?" I am grateful that I had the courage to follow my heart because I just *knew* it was the right decision for me. My children were also concerned as to where the money was going to come from. I rented out one of the bedrooms in my new home and the money came in every month, enabling me to pay my rent on time.

Spirit always guides me when I'm making a decision through open and closed doors. If I am not sure if it's the right path for me, I ask Spirit to open or close the door. As I walk in faith, it always works and there have been many times when the door was closed at the last minute! I'm so grateful that God opened the door for my dream home.

I said to my son, Tim, after I moved in, "How did I get here?"

He said, "Mom, you have been talking about living on the water for as long as I can remember." It was my dream to live on the water and I didn't care if it was a pond, a lake, a puddle, or the ocean!

I lived alone in my dream house for one year before Larry moved in. Larry and I have lived in the house together now for five years. We love it so much and cannot believe where the time has gone. We have no idea how long we will be here, so we enjoy and appreciate every minute of every day.

We were married a year after he moved in. I love being married to Larry and he truly is an answer to my prayers. We love and support one another and encourage each other to be vessels of Love wherever we go. We enjoy being retired and doing whatever we want when we want to. Life is good and we are grateful.

Never give up on your dreams. Keep believing and trusting in God's timing. God has placed your desires in your heart and will answer your prayers in divine timing. If it happened to me, it can and will happen to you.

Faith

Larry:

Pat and I had been discussing moving in together for some time. I had been living alone for the past three years and was perfectly happy in my condo. The thought of moving was not pleasant, even though Pat and I were very compatible and loved being together. Like many people, I don't necessarily like change, so it was a big decision for me to make. If I hadn't decided to take a chance and commit to a serious relationship, we wouldn't be where we are now, living together and married.

Even though I felt some fear, it seemed like the right thing to do. I am learning not to worry and control things, but to allow Spirit to do the work. I am also learning to choose Love instead of fear. During this process, I realized how much of my decision making over the years has been fear based. I often tortured myself with thoughts like, "If I do this, I'm afraid this will happen and if I don't do that, I'm afraid that will happen." Fear based ego can make your life a nightmare.

I didn't manifest very often because I didn't understand what it was all about. In difficult times, I would ask for God's help, yet it never really felt like I received any help. Today, I am living with one of the great manifestors. I was a bit skeptical at first, but all you have to do is see Pat in action and you cannot deny her ability to practice her faith in a very real way. When she wants something, she just puts it out there, and sooner or later she receives her request. She manifested our relationship, the house we live in, the happiness we enjoy, and even parking spaces.

Pat has convinced me to *believe* before *I see*. I find myself getting parking spaces all the time just by asking, being grateful, and expecting the parking space to be there. I look forward every day to God's little surprises.

Pat and I practice and support one another regarding our financial future. We know millionaires who struggle with not having enough money and are fearful they will run out of resources before they die. I wonder if most or all people struggle with this "not enough money syndrome". I know we do at times, especially when an unexpected bill comes in. When we become fearful at these times, we remind one another to live in the moment because all we have is *now*. The future is not here until it becomes the present.

When I finally made the decision that the move was for my highest good and for the good of our relationship, everything seemed to just fall into place. Our mantra or prayer was, "Everything will flow with peace, ease, and grace." Whenever I felt anxious about the move, Pat reminded me about the mantra, and we would say it together. It really worked because "we get what we expect" and I was expecting it to flow with peace, ease, and grace.

Here are a couple of examples: I felt concerned about who would help me move the furniture and heavy stuff from my condo. I really valued and respected the relationship I had with my landlords. When I gave them the notice that I was leaving, they were disappointed. To my surprise, without even asking they said, "We have a truck and would be happy to move you to your new home." The move went, as we expected, with peace, ease, and grace. I'm not a "techie" and was concerned about setting up my computer and smart TV. My landlord and his wife not only helped me move, but they set up my computer and TV on the same day.

I wanted to purchase a new Stressless recliner I had seen at the furniture store that I really liked. Unfortunately, it was beyond my budget and retailed at 2000 dollars. The next day, Pat checked out Craigslist and sure enough, there was a Stressless recliner for sale. Not only was it in my budget for 800 dollars, but it looked brand new and they lived right in our area. When I sat in it, my body relaxed, and I knew this was the recliner for me. We didn't know how we were going to get it home because we didn't have a truck. The owner was a young, strong man and said, "I would be happy to deliver the recliner with my truck." Not only did he deliver the recliner to our home, but he carried it in and set it up. We really appreciated his kindness and generosity. I am now enjoying the recliner every day and love it.

I am settling into my new "home" and enjoying our free and easy Stressless lifestyle. My heart is full of gratitude for what Love has brought into my life. I am happy and look forward to walking this path of Love with Pat as we grow spiritually as a couple and as individuals. We are given many opportunities every day to grow and become more conscious. Sometimes that's scary, but it's nice to know someone has my back. I look forward to continuing this journey and welcoming all the opportunities that will arise.

I am grateful for Pat who has been a loving and helpful example of accepting the light and energy of Love, and encourages me to experience the God that is Love. All we have to do is open our hearts to Love, and to the extent that we can do that, we will become who we are meant to be.

JOURNAL

When have I stepped out in faith and what happened?

Do I feel guided by Spirit when making a decision?

Do I trust God's timing in my life?

Chapter 21

Fear

"To overcome fear, here's all you have to do: realize the fear is there,
and do the action you fear anyway."
~ Peter McWilliams

Larry:

Do we realize how much we allow fear to affect our lives? How often do we allow fear to determine what decisions we make or don't make? Fear is so insidious and hides so completely that we don't even know it's there inside of us making our lives miserable. The more we allow fear to go unrecognized, the worse it gets. Have you ever been in a situation where you just can't make a decision and you don't know why?

When I sold my catering business, I was forty-five years old and had to find a way to make a living. I didn't want to admit it, but fear was my constant companion. I felt frightened and alone. I was going through a divorce after twenty-one years of marriage and had to find a new place to live and get used to living alone. I struggled with this because my life had changed so dramatically in a short time. It's very difficult for a man to admit that he's afraid because we are taught to be strong, macho, and the protectors. Fear is viewed as weak and shameful.

I think many men push fear down and medicate it with one addiction or another. We are often not even aware that it is fear related. After a while, I thought, "Perhaps I'd like to meet someone but dating over the last twenty-one years had really changed. Being twenty years older didn't help with my self-confidence either." Just the thought of dating was scary. Did I want to put myself out there, become vulner-able and take the risk of getting hurt again? I struggled through that and at times it wasn't pretty, but I persevered and eventually, I became comfortable with the single life and dating again. As I look back at those years, I think it could have been a lot easier if I had the consciousness that I have today.

What I didn't realize back then was that I had a choice. There is another power available to us that is stronger than fear, more powerful than anything created by humankind, that is the power of Love! We don't have to go through life's difficulties alone and allow fear to paralyze us.

I have learned that Love is the energy and light of God. Love is offered to us every moment of every day. We can't earn it because it is a gift just waiting to be accepted. I can choose fear or I can choose Love. I know this sounds simple and it is, but it's not easy. I had to stop thinking that I wasn't worthy or good enough to receive Love.

Like most of us, I've made mistakes in my life and, at times, felt like I haven't measured up. How many of you have felt that way? I learned that Love is never a question of worthiness. We just need to be open to receive the unconditional gift that is being offered.

You may want to try this response the next time you feel fear threatening you. I say something like this, "I am not accepting fear in this situation, I delete all fearful thoughts, I choose the power of Love. I delete fear and choose Love, I delete fear and choose Love." Repeat this as often as you need too. I hope you find this helpful. Love has never let me down. The next time fear presents itself in your life, what will you choose?

Fear

Pat:

After thirty years of marriage, raising four children and being a stay-at-home mom, it was a big step of faith to ask for a divorce. I was filled with *fear*. I got married when I was twenty-one and had never lived alone. My husband took care of the finances. I remember how nervous I was opening my first savings account. The teller was so kind and walked me through every step of the way.

We didn't have a bad marriage and from the outside, it looked like we were the perfect family. We didn't fight and supported one another the best we could. We were both raised in severe alcoholic homes and had no idea what we were doing. We worked hard to communicate and raise our children with healthy values.

I went into therapy when I was in my late thirties. I started the process of finding myself and healing childhood sexual abuse, clergy sexual abuse, and parental alcoholism. It was a long journey, but I was determined to get healthy and be the woman God created me to be.

I was a people pleaser and focused on fixing and taking care of others, including my husband. I didn't want to look at my behaviors and the pain that was inside of me. As I got healthier and became more assertive and started to speak up, my husband was threatened and didn't like the new me.

I went back to school and earned a bachelor's degree, which was a miracle because I didn't think I could do it. In fact, I dropped out of school for a year because I was filled with fear and didn't think I could write a twenty page paper. Facing my fear was huge, but I did it and finished school. A few years later, I earned my master's degree. This enabled me to get a great job as an alcohol and drug therapist at the VA Medical Center and provide for myself. When I retired from the VA fourteen years ago, I became a Certified Spiritual Life Coach.

I was fifty-two years old when I got a divorce. I remember saying to myself, "I don't want to be seventy years old and wished I had gotten a divorce sooner." I wanted to live my life to the fullest and knew deep down, I couldn't do that if I stay married. We were on different paths and it just wasn't going to work.

Another example where I had to face and conquer my fear was writing my first book. God had been "hounding" me for over twenty-five years to write my book, *Simply a Woman of Faith*. Facing my fears and believing in myself has been a journey of self-discovery and deepened faith. I would write for months at a time and then stop writing for a year because I became discouraged.

I cried myself to sleep one night because I was so full of fear about writing a book. I had no idea what I was doing, I thought no one would read it and I was wasting my time. I believe God communicates to us in many ways if we are open to listening and accepting guidance. It may be through dreams, other people, books, intuition, or synchro-nicities, etc.

I had a powerful dream that night. I was walking up the stairs to heaven and when I got to the top, I reached out to touch a star and then became the *star*. I saw this as a confirmation that it was God's plan for me to write a book.

At one point in the journey, I said to God, "You have chosen the wrong person, I'm not doing it." When people asked me how the book was coming, I answered, "I put the book to bed." End of story.

This pattern of starting and stopping writing went on for six years until I got serious about my writing, changed my thinking, and took steps to make it happen.

One year after I stopped writing my book, while preparing for the retreat I was leading, "Love is Letting Go of Fear", God showed me clearly that I was stuck in *fear* and that was the real reason I put the "book to bed". I really didn't want to admit this to myself or others that it was fear that prevented me from writing my book.

I questioned my faith often during the process of writing. Faith is knowing I'm being guided and given everything I need to accomplish the task. I often felt overwhelmed and didn't think I had enough faith.

"God, I'm feeling afraid, overwhelmed, and alone. Why did you choose me to write a book? I'm not a businesswoman. I know nothing about publishing and marketing. I'm in over my head. I'm afraid of making the wrong decisions. I need help."

100

The day after asking God for help, I went to work with a heavy heart, trying to shake off the negativity and fear that was lodged in my body. I picked up a Peoples magazine to throw it away in the conference room. Instead of throwing it away, I just opened it to a page and couldn't believe my eyes. *I have a plan that will make all your dreams come true.*

I sat down, put my head on the table, and cried like a baby. I needed God's heavenly touch to get me back on track and continue to write when I wanted to give up.

As God promised, everything I needed was provided as I let go and trusted in the Divine Plan. My book was published in 2007. If I had not faced my fears, I would not be living my dream on Maui and happily married.

Larry and I started writing our book three years ago and finished it during the pandemic. During this time, I fell on a rock and broke my shoulder while walking on the beach. I was alone and it was early in the morning. There wasn't another person in sight. I was in a lot of pain and couldn't get up as the waves crashed on me. As the fear enveloped me, I started to repeat, "I choose Love." It was in no time when I noticed a man walking toward me on the beach. I called out to him and asked for help. He was my angel. Circumstances developed where I was transported home and later received medical attention at the emergency clinic.

I still struggle with fear sometimes when I don't live in the present moment and think about the future: my health, living alone, finances. The difference is I recognize it almost immediately and know what to do. My ego wants me to feel fear and blame others.

I allow myself to feel the fear for as long as I need to and then let it go and "choose Love". Love is always the answer and will give me everything I need.

JOURNAL

Do I allow fear to control my life in making decisions?

Am I open to the power of Love to not allow fear to paralyze me?

Where am I stuck and unable to move forward?

Chapter 22

Flexibility

"Stay committed to your decisions, but stay flexible in your approach."
~ Tony Robbins

Pat:

One of the reasons my relationship with Larry works so well and why I love it so much is because we have learned to be *flexible* with life and with one another. In other words, we are learning to go with the flow and accept "what is". It seems like a theme in our lives these days is to surrender and accept "what is" because we need to practice it daily if we want to experience peace.

I don't think being flexible in a relationship is easy or even doable if you haven't learned to be flexible and to trust what you need to do for yourself in each moment. For example, I really looked forward to attending a potluck luncheon with my yoga group on Memorial Day. Larry and I both had busy weeks and I helped a friend move into her new home. I spent Sunday "filling myself up" by being quiet and resting, which was good for my soul and exactly what I needed.

I felt surprised when I went to bed that I started to feel "uncomfortable" about attending the yoga luncheon on Memorial Day because I was really looking forward to it. I didn't understand why I didn't want to go and, of course, I didn't want to disappoint my friends. I have learned to go within and trust Spirit that I am being guided and will do what is right and for my highest good.

There was a time in my life that I wouldn't give myself permission to change my mind just because I wanted to. If I was sick, that wouldn't be a problem saying no to what I said I would do. But to change my mind, and not follow through is something I didn't do because I was more concerned about what others would think of me.

It took me a long time to decide and then I would have to talk myself out of feeling guilty.

I am grateful for my growth and how I have learned to respect my wants and needs and take care of myself in body, mind, and spirit. I have learned to change my mind and say no without guilt.

Instead of attending the yoga luncheon, Larry and I decided to spend the day together driving up-country and going out to lunch. This felt more peaceful since we hadn't spent much time together during the week. A few hours later, the desire to spend the day on the road just didn't feel peaceful. I wanted to stay home and just *be*.

When I shared it with Larry, he was flexible and fine with it, which I knew he would be. He loves to stay home and relax. He respected my need for quiet and was willing to change his plans. Within a few minutes, he received a phone call from the people renting the condo he manages and had to address the problem immediately. If we had pressured ourselves to go up-country, we would have had to turn around and go back home to address the problem at the condo.

I would not want to be in a relationship with someone if I wasn't respected and there wasn't flexibility, especially at this time in my life. Of course, there are times when I choose to do something for a person I love that I don't particularly want to do. The difference is that it is a matter of choice and I am doing it out of love rather than guilt and trying to please someone.

Spirit has taught me to trust my intuition when making decisions and to know I will always be guided by the energy and light of Love.

Flexibility

Larry:

I have a practice of starting each day with a heart full of gratitude for all that I have been given, especially for the gifts of kindness and patience. I sometimes feel like I take one step forward and two steps back when it comes to kindness and patience. It's my experience that the gift never comes in the way I expect it too. The opportunity to be patient or kind is usually a surprise and there are times when I don't even recognize the "gift" as an opportunity.

I consider the experience that "Sparkle" (my nickname for Pat) shared with you about her dance shoes from Saturday evening as an opportunity and gift. It seems like "ego" is always ready to jump into action in a heartbeat. I could have really gone off and said some negative things to Pat. I am beginning to remember, in situations that can be stressful, that I have choices. I need to make positive choices when things don't always go the way I'm expecting them to go. It's so easy to go right to blame, condemnation, and judgment.

Was I happy that we had to go all the way home to get her shoes? No, I wasn't happy, but really, it's not the end of the world. Someone I love made a mistake and it was time for me to be flexible, forgiving, and understanding. I was reminded, "to be careful about what you pray for because you just may get it."

We had an interesting experience when we returned to our home to retrieve Pat's shoes. Our neighbor across the street has three dogs. They bark constantly throughout the day and sometimes into the night. A couple of weeks ago, I ran into this neighbor as I returned from my morning walk. I approached her and introduced myself. I asked her, "Could you please contain your dogs from barking so much."

She said, "I will try."

I am pleased to say that she has done something, and the barking has been reduced by ninety percent. As we were leaving our home after getting Pat's shoes, I saw our neighbor working in her yard. I stopped the car and said, "I really appreciate whatever you have done to reduce the dogs barking."

She smiled and said, "Thank You." I think she was generally pleased with our appreciation.

Who knows, perhaps that whole scenario with Pat's shoes happened so we could show our appreciation to our neighbor. I remembered Pat saying, "There is a reason."

Love consciousness is teaching me to choose Love rather than ego. It is my responsibility to remember that in all situations I have a choice. I can choose Love or fear.

JOURNAL

Do I go with the flow, am I able to be flexible?

Am I able to choose Love instead of fear?

Do I try to control instead of being flexible with my partner?

Chapter 23

Forgiveness

*"Forgiveness simply means loving someone enough to pursue healing
instead of punishment when they have wronged you."*
~ Dave Willis

Larry:

There have been times in my life when I have been hurt and broken
right down to the core. I tried to live my life according to the beliefs
of my faith and had allowed the church to take responsibility for my
life. All I had to do was obey the rules and I would get to heaven. My
life was crumbling all around me, even though I tried to obey all the
rules. I was married for twenty-one years with two children. In the
last few years of my marriage, I felt so alone, unloved, and unappre-
ciated. I realized we were on two different paths and it was clear it
wasn't going to work anymore. I had to forgive myself for not being
able to salvage my marriage. After my divorce, I felt like I had failed
my wife and my children.

I searched and prayed for help, it seemed that God had
abandoned me. *Or so I thought.* I finally said to God "if this is the way
it's going to be when I am doing my best to be a good Christian, screw
you I'm better off on my own." I had nothing to do with God for over
ten years. I was angry at God and blamed Him for things happening in
my life that I didn't like. I felt like a rudderless boat bobbing in the
ocean. During the years of suffering and pain, I wasn't able to see it as
part of my spiritual journey.

I had so much to learn about myself. Looking back at those
turbulent years, I have a better understanding of how God was helping
me even when I didn't feel like He was. I had to experience those
terrible, sad, frustrating, lonely days in order to break the mold my
belief structure had created.

I see things so differently now, I fully accept responsibility for my relationship with my God, who is not somewhere out "there" waiting to punish me if I don't live up to his rules. My God is a God of "Love" which resides in me and in every person.

As I began to take responsibility for my life, I began to think for myself. I made decisions by asking myself, "What would Jesus do in each decision I made?" I was now able to discover the spiritual relationship with God that was being offered to me. God was giving me the opportunity for a whole new different walk in faith, where all my questions were addressed and answered. For the last fifty years, I have been on this path and it has brought me to the conclusion that "Love is God."

Forgiveness is one of the most difficult disciplines to practice. When we have hurt another or someone has hurt us, it's difficult to understand the importance of forgiveness. I had a difficult time trying to forgive myself or others until "Love" showed me how. I believe that "Love" does not judge, hold grudges, or keeps score. "Love" is egoless. The ego wants us to stay separated and angry at people and situations that have hurt us. The ego sustains itself with anger, resentment, blame, judgment, and drama. The ego perpetuates racist thinking, encouraging us to believe that we are better than someone else and they are lesser because of color, beliefs, or economic status. The unhappier we are, the happier the ego is.

Once I learned that forgiveness doesn't mean that I condone what has been done to me, I found it easier to forgive. Making the *decision* to forgive is the first step in forgiving. When I first decide to forgive someone, it doesn't feel like I'm forgiving them. Of course, the ego doesn't want us to forgive and tries to persuade us that the situation doesn't warrant forgiveness. Once we realize the ego is trying to sabotage our desire to forgive, we can turn to Love for assistance. I ask Love to show me the way and I listen to what Love tells me.

When I'm unwilling to forgive, it doesn't hurt the person I'm angry with. It's a poison that affects my whole being. By holding onto negative experiences and anger, I cannot move on with my life and receive the healing grace that Love wants to give me.

We all make mistakes on this journey of life and sometimes the one we need to forgive is ourselves. Forgiving myself has been the most difficult part of my journey. I say to myself, "You could have tried harder, made better decisions, been more patient, more understanding, or less selfish." Then I remember that whatever I did at that moment was the best I could do at that time. As we learn to forgive ourselves, it becomes easier to forgive others.

Another belief I had was that I needed to blame someone and make them wrong so I would be right. I know now that blaming others is a tool of the ego to keep me from forgiving. Once the ego is recognized, it begins to lose its power. The more I'm able to accept Love's energy and light, the more easily I am able to recognize the ego.

I'm hoping you will have the courage to work on forgiveness in your life so you can experience the joy and peacefulness of a soul not burdened from unforgiveness. Let Love show you the way. When someone shoots an arrow at you, stop it before it enters your heart. Turn it into a beautiful flower, then return it to sender with love.

Forgiveness

Pat:

I had to forgive myself for my mistakes and I had to forgive my alcoholic parents who neglected me due to their disease.

It was a long and hard road uncovering and discovering the truth of who I am as a divine spiritual being. I was willing to do whatever I needed to do to heal and recover from childhood sexual abuse and family dysfunction.

I was sexually abused by a Catholic priest in my early teens. This could have turned me away from God. Instead, I drew closer to God and drew my strength from Source. I blocked the memories of the abuse for many years until I attended a professional workshop about clergy sexual abuse. It all started to come back to me. I joined a survivor group and did the inner work of forgiveness and letting go. We can either become bitter or better. I chose to become better.

I have learned that forgiveness is for me, not the other person. I am not condoning another's actions, but I am setting myself free of resentments, blame, and anger. Forgiveness is a gift I give myself.

It takes courage and a willingness to dig deep and face the truth about ourselves and our past. We must take responsibility for ourselves and not blame and judge others. We must forgive ourselves and others if we are going to move forward and live the life we are intended to live. Forgiveness is a process and takes time. It's tempting to want to forgive prematurely, rather than go through the grief process and feel all of our feelings.

When memories started to surface that my father sexually abused me as a child, I didn't want to feel the anger and sadness that was buried deep inside of me. I loved my father and was always daddy's little girl.

In my first session with the therapist, I said, "I'm ready to forgive my father. I know he was drunk when he abused me and didn't mean it."

She looked at me with compassion and patience and said, "You are not ready to forgive, you must go through the process before you get to acceptance and forgiveness."

I'm grateful for her wisdom and my willingness to listen and do the inner work. It wasn't easy. I believe it was the grace of God to endure, as it took me three years to work through the abuse before I was ready to forgive my father.

Here is another example of where I was able to forgive. I experienced changes this past year in a relationship with a soul sister that has been painful and difficult. I thought we were forever heart-friends. She didn't want to be friends anymore because I had changed too much. We were on different spiritual paths and she appeared to be threatened. I understand that there are seasons and not every relationship is forever because our needs and desires change.

I allowed myself to process all of my feelings: sadness, grief, hurt, disappointment, and anger with the loss of my friend. I chose to take responsibility for my part in the relationship and not blame her or hold resentment. It took courage and trust to believe it wasn't good or bad. I didn't take it personally or blame myself for what happened.

With the grace of God, and my willingness to forgive, I was able to move beyond the pain and hurt and send her love. I am choosing to love her unconditionally. I pray for her daily and continue to hold her close in my heart. The value of suffering is to *wake us up* so we can choose Love. I am choosing Love because Love is all there is. You forgive to the extent that you love. Forgiveness is the best form of Love. It takes a strong person to say they are sorry and an even stronger person to forgive.

How about you? What are you choosing today? Are you in resistance to some change in your life or are you able to accept "what is" and trust the Divine has a plan for your life?

I encourage you to ask for help if you need it. Remember, it is a sign of *strength*, not *weakness*. You are worth it and deserve to live a peaceful and abundant life.

JOURNAL

Have I ever felt like God abandoned me?

Do I accept responsibility for my relationship with God?

Am I able to forgive myself?

Do I blame others, am I unable to forgive?

Chapter 24

Giving and Receiving

"We make a living by what we get. We make a life by what we give."
~ *Winston S. Churchill*

Larry:

I shared with Pat an experience I had many years ago that taught me a very important lesson about giving with no strings attached.

Thirty years ago, I worked in a soup kitchen one day a week. We provided and cooked meals for around one hundred people. One evening in February on a snowy subzero night, I noticed a man come in the building with just a light sweater on. He was wet, shivering, and looked like he was on his last leg. I couldn't believe he was out in these winter elements without a coat or jacket.

I had worn my favorite tan winter parka with a fur collar around the hood. I loved it because it was the warmest parka I had ever owned. After I noticed the man, I thought, "I just can't let him go out on a night like this without a coat." I gave him my parka. He thanked me and appeared to appreciate my gift.

Half an hour later, I couldn't believe it when I saw the man wearing an old ratty jacket and the parka, I had given him was gone. I felt angry and betrayed. I thought, "What's the matter with you, are you crazy? I gave my beautiful new parka away for nothing."

From my perspective, he had traded it and made an extremely poor bargain.

Later in the evening while I was thinking about this experience, I asked myself some serious questions about my giving practices.

- Did I give the man a gift?
- Did it have strings attached?

- Do I give gifts with expectations? If the parka was a gift, he could do what he wanted to do with it.
- Does he have to use the gift according to my wishes?
- It was no longer mine; it's gone, out of my life.

One of the gifts I received was that I was compassionate, generous, and loving to a man I didn't even know. I gave him something that was especially important to me to make his life a little better.

The other lesson I learned and haven't forgotten thirty years later is that when I give a gift, there are no expectations or strings attached. My joy is in the giving and you receiving.

Giving and Receiving

Pat:

Do you agree with this? There is more joy in giving than receiving? I think it needs to be both to live a balanced life. I don't believe we can really receive without the experience of giving and we can't give without the experience of receiving. Like many of us, I am more comfortable with giving, as it gives me great joy to help others.

This chapter in my life is about receiving. I fell on a rock while walking on the beach and broke my shoulder. My heart has been cracked open because of the love and support I have received from Larry, my children, and friends here on Maui. Friends brought us meals, shopped at the farmers market, and brought me flowers. I asked for prayers from friends on Facebook and the response has been overwhelming. I know I'm healing quickly and with minimal pain because of everyone's prayers and love.

I'm allowing myself to ask for what I need and be vulnerable. At this moment in time, there are things I cannot do for myself with a broken right shoulder and have to ask for help. It is humbling to realize I am not in control of my life, even though at times, I think I am.

We never know what the next moment will bring, do we? It is my intention to be peaceful with whatever is happening around me. I am at peace when I'm grateful, accept "what is" and live in the present moment. I am given the opportunity to practice what I believe; everything happens for a reason. I can become bitter and complain or become better and evolve. I am not alone as Love always provides, guides, and protects me.

When people ask me how they can help, I swallow my pride and respond honestly, "We would really appreciate a home cooked meal if you would like to do something for us." When I ask others how I can help them, it's a joy when they are free enough to tell me what they need. It takes out the guessing and gives me the opportunity to serve them

115

JOURNAL

Am I able to give without expectations or strings attached?

Can I be vulnerable and ask for what I want?

Am I able to receive from others?

Chapter 25

Gratitude

"When we focus on our gratitude, the tide of disappointment goes out and the tide of love rushes in."
~ Kristin Armstrong

Pat:

Gratitude, being an element of Love, provides us with opportunities to express our appreciation for all the gifts we receive daily. It's a conscious decision to live in gratitude when we want to complain about situations that we have no control over. By choosing an attitude of gratitude, we experience a life filled with peace, joy, and happiness.

Larry and I decided to take a two week cruise to Sydney, Australia. I love being on the ocean and looked forward to relaxing and enjoying our time together. I made the decision before I left to completely "unplug" from the world, which meant no phone, email, texts, or Facebook for two weeks. I knew I would miss it, but I didn't want anything to distract me from "living in the moment" and my time with Larry. I felt excited because I sensed it was going to be a powerful time together. My intention was to relax, be peaceful and in the moment, have fun, pray, play, rest, enjoy, dance, and be a vessel of Love. I experienced all of the above and more.

After we arrived on the MS *Noordam* and got settled into our room, I immediately started a gratitude book that I wrote in daily. Larry and I made a commitment to one another that we would not complain about anything but be grateful for everything that happened.

I journaled daily so I was able to look back over the days and see what transpired for me. Although there were many things to be grateful for, we had lots of "opportunities" to practice our commitment not to complain about anything. There are always lessons to be learned in life and it takes practice to become a master at what you are learning.

We were learning about living in the *now* because everything happens in the present moment. The next minute is not promised. I asked myself, "Do I want to waste this precious moment complaining because I don't like what's happening or will I choose to be grateful, knowing that whatever is happening is a gift and opportunity to grow and learn?"

After only five days of cruising on the ocean, I woke up feeling a sense of "boredom". I missed Maui, my girlfriends, my painting, and my phone! I tried not to judge myself. (A cruise of a lifetime with my beloved and I am feeling bored, what is wrong with you girl?) I shared it with Larry, and he had just finished reading something from Eckhart Tolle's book *Stillness Speaks* that talked about boredom. Tolle wrote, "Just feel it, just like you would feel sadness or anger. Go into it, rather than giving it meaning, because it's not you."

As I sat with it and prayed about it, I realized that I am fearful when I have nothing to do or nothing planned, even though I love the days where nothing is planned and I allow the day to unfold naturally. I still feel some anxiety when I don't know what the next thing I am going to do is rather than enjoying the moment, living in the *now*, and going with the flow. I asked myself, "Is this about my need to control and needing to know what's next?" It definitely was.

Since living on Maui, I have been practicing going with the flow and living in the moment, so I was surprised to see there was more healing that I needed. It feels like I am being invited to a deeper level of *being*, trusting, and letting go of control.

We really enjoyed the cruise, especially the food, staff, and entertainment. We spent many hours just being together, dancing, reading, and loving one another.

One of the highlights for me was winning the cruise line's version of "Dancing with the Stars". After many hours of practicing, and learning the dance, it was a thrill to perform with my dance partner in front of a few thousand people. I really felt like a *star*.

I was given the opportunity to not complain when the strap on my dance shoe broke *right before* we were to perform. How easy it would have been for me to panic, complain, and feel like a victim. Instead, I chose to accept the situation and trusted that Love energy would provide for me. I was very grateful that the dance company provided me with a pair of dance shoes. Although the heel on the shoes were much higher than I was used to wearing and I wasn't sure if I could dance in them, I took a deep breath, smiled, and trusted I wouldn't fall on my face in front of the audience. To my surprise and delight, I danced gracefully and had a ball.

It feels like something has "shifted" inside of me since the cruise and I don't know what it is, but I know something is different. I am giving myself time to process it. Since I have come home, I feel more peaceful and relaxed. I haven't hit the ground running like I always do when I return from a trip.

I believe this shift happened because I was open to practicing gratitude rather than being negative and complaining about all the challenges that occurred on our cruise.

Gratitude

Larry:

We had a wonderful time on our cruise, but I am so happy to be home. I've discovered that I'm not a true blue traveler and missed our home on Maui.

Pat shared that we had decided not to complain about anything, but to stay in a place of gratitude, acceptance, and peace. A few occasions arose that truly challenged me to practice this.

The first opportunity not to complain was when I started to get a sore throat after being on the cruise for five days that turned into a full-blown cold and cough. My response to that in the past would have been, "Poor me, I paid all this money on a cruise anticipating a wonderful time and I get sick." But I didn't go there and didn't complain. Then Pat got sick, which was kind of expected. She also stayed positive and was able to function well. We spent lots of time reading, relaxing, and spending quality time together, which is exactly what the doctor ordered.

In Eckhart Tolle's book *Stillness Speaks*, he suggests that we are not our thoughts, we are not our sickness or trials—we are "who" is aware of them. He invites us not to take our thoughts seriously, not to own our sickness or trials, and not hold onto them. He encourages us to go through them to the other side, to awareness. With these intentions in mind, this is what I did when I got sick and started to feel better after one day. Pat spoke to the doctor on the ship and he said, "These coughs are lasting for seven-to-fourteen days and mine lasted for six months."

The second opportunity to be grateful happened as we were disembarking from the ship. We walked through an area where a woman was selling handmade leis. It's not my practice to purchase items like this at all, but I noticed a beautiful carved wooden lei that I had never seen before. I decided to purchase it for myself. When I reached into my pocket to get my wallet, I found that I had forgotten it in the safe on the ship, along with our passports and plane tickets. If I hadn't decided to stop and purchase the lei, we would not have known that we left our valuables in the safe on the ship

If we had left the secure area, we would not have been able to get back on the ship. Therefore, we would not have had our plane tickets, passports, or money. Instead of complaining that we forgot our valuables, we accepted the situation as a gift. We felt like we had been guided and protected.

The third opportunity to be grateful and not complain was after we disembarked from the ship at eight am. The taxi picked us up to take us to our hotel. Our flight back to Maui was at nine-thirty pm, so we were looking forward to spending the day touring Sydney. We booked a hotel for the day through Travelocity so we could relax and take a shower before our ten hour flight back home.

The taxi driver drove around in circles trying to find the hotel (as I watched his meter going higher and higher.) It was hard to believe there was no hotel when we arrived at the address given to us.

We tried calling the hotel, but there was no answer. There we were at nine in the morning with six suitcases and no hotel for us to stay. It would have been so easy for me to feel angry, frustrated, and fearful, but I didn't go there. I was able to almost see the comedic aspect of the whole thing as I looked over at Pat with her eyes closed repeating, "Everything is flowing with peace, ease, and grace."

The cab driver didn't know what to do and randomly pulled over to the curb and right in front of us was another hotel. I walked into the hotel and asked the manager, "Do you have a room available?"

He said, "Yes, but you are lucky because we were completely booked for Friday and Saturday and we just had a cancellation, so you are in luck." We were thrilled that we were able to get a room right away at the same price we had paid for at the phantom hotel.

We made plans with the same taxi driver, Sam, to pick us up at seven pm and drive us to the airport for our flight at nine-thirty pm. We enjoyed the day exploring Sydney and having a delicious lunch. We were able to take a shower and relax before our ten hour flight back to Maui.

We waited for Sam in front of the hotel until seven-fifteen pm, but he never showed up. We didn't panic and become fearful. We just called another taxi company that arrived in ten minutes and off we went racing to the airport. Again, we didn't complain and didn't allow fear, frustration, or anger to enter our energy. On the way to the airport, I turned to Pat and said, "We have to send Sam love and forgiveness" and she agreed.

JOURNAL

Do I express gratitude and appreciation for what I have in my life?

Do I complain when things don't go my way?

Can I let the day unfold without plans?

Chapter 26

Honesty

"Whomever is careless with the truth in small matters
cannot be trusted with important matters."
~ *Albert Einstein*

Pat:

Larry and I love being retired. He does what he wants to do during the day, and I do what I want to do and we come together at night to relax and share about the day. We take day trips and go out to breakfast and lunch often. We dance, pray, play, and are writing our book together. He likes to stay home more than I do, and I like to play with the girls. I like my quiet time and have my "Pat" days when I want to. In other words, we give each other the *freedom* to do what is important to both of us. It works for us as we are creating a "conscious" love relationship and are enjoying the fruits of our labor. We are remembering that we are all connected and there is only Love.

We do have a major difference that we are working on and we strive to be respectful of one another. We know that neither one of us is right nor wrong, simply different perspectives. I like "stuff" which he thinks is "clutter". I have candles and flowers and pretty things around the house. He has been great with giving me the freedom to decorate the way I want to because it didn't seem to matter to him. Larry is more of a minimalist and prefers not to have things around, especially in the kitchen. Perhaps because he was in the food industry for many years, he likes things to be organized and I try to be sensitive to that.

When I moved into our current home six and a half years ago, it was fully furnished, and I had my own stuff that I had accumulated. When Larry moved in a year and a half later, he brought his belongings. There is little storage room in our home and things got stuffed into the kitchen cabinets. I managed to organize it, so everything was in its place, or so I thought.

It all came to a head when I heard the crash of glass in the kitchen. I came running in from outside to see what happened. There was glass all over the floor and counters. Larry was terribly upset and yelled, "I am so f— frustrated with this clutter." I had never seen him so angry and it scared me because he is usually very calm.

Instead of staying there and helping him clean up the glass which I would have done in the past to make everything ok, I immediately went back outside to calm myself down. I am grateful that I had the presence of mind to *keep my mouth shut and not argue.* I sat outside praying and feeling my feelings. When I came in from outside an hour later, I went into the room to discuss what happened. Larry said, "I have a letter to write on my computer and left the room." I assumed he wasn't ready to talk about what happened. I went to the other bedroom and rested and read.

What upset me, other than the fact that he was so angry, is that I didn't have any idea that he felt so frustrated and strongly about the "clutter" as he called it. *I wasn't willing to take responsibility for something I didn't know about.* He had a responsibility to lovingly share with me things that were bothering him. An hour later, he came into the room and kind of apologized, but minimized what happened and said, "I don't want to make a big deal out of this."

It was a big deal because I had never seen him like that, and he scared the s— out of me. I also wondered if there were other things that bothered him that he wasn't talking about.

The next morning when we talked about it, Larry said, "I didn't realize how much the kitchen cabinets bothered me until the glass shattered all over the place. I don't want to complain about everything, so I usually just ignore things." I was quiet and listened to him as he shared his perspective. "I'm lazy and could have done something about the cabinets if I didn't like them or I could have talked to you about them before I exploded."

I said, "I am also lazy and instead of taking things out that we weren't using, I kept putting more things in." Larry agreed when he becomes aware that something is bothering him, he will let me know and not ignore it. I agreed to not put anything in the cabinet unless I take something out.

It is my belief that Spirit uses everything for our highest good. Since the "crash" there is a fire under my butt to clean out other cabinets that have things stuffed into them. It really feels lighter.

We are learning to be open with one other. Love energy is showing us how to be respectful of each other's perspectives by encouraging us to be patient, honest, and flexible.

Honesty

Larry:

This was a great opportunity to address a situation where we both had different perspectives. Pat loves paintings and pictures and there isn't much room on our walls for anymore. She also likes rocks, crystals, statues, and flowers. She receives great satisfaction and peace from having all these things around the house. She loves to go out Saturday mornings to garage sales to find treasures and I encourage her to go and have fun.

This week, I realized I wasn't fine with the cabinets after the bowl crashed on the counter. We have little storage space; our kitchen cabinets are packed jam full of plates, bowl, cups, and glasses.

I had just gotten up from a late nap and was still kind of groggy. When I opened the kitchen cabinet door and reached for a bowl, a dish fell out and crashed into a million pieces on the counter. I was shocked and startled. My comfort level went from a calm level of zero to an alarming level of 1000. I felt angry at being startled. I proceeded to clean up the mess and started to calm down. I knew I needed to be alone for a while. Pat had never seen me this angry, so it was upsetting and scary for her.

As I took the time to think about what happened, I realized that I wasn't upset with Pat, but I was upset with myself. I take responsibility for placing all the cups, glasses, plates back into the cabinets because the cabinets are high and it's easier for me to reach than it is for Pat. I had been living under these circumstances for more than two and a half years and wondered why I didn't do something about it up until now? The truth is, it wasn't important enough and I was just too lazy to do or say anything about it.

Pat encouraged me to speak up when things bother me rather than let them build up and then explode. I really didn't know it was bothering me until the crash. I work at being flexible and not complaining. I agreed to be honest and speak up, and not see it as complaining.

The next morning, we discussed what happened and what we could do to resolve it. I had the idea to buy some big plastic bins and put the things we are not using into them. We spent the morning going through the cabinets and cleaning them out. Sometimes, I'm not the brightest bulb in the package because I never even thought of doing that until now. The lesson I learned is to pay attention if something is bothering me rather than ignore it before I blow my cool. I'll do better the next time. Pat agreed to not put anything new in the kitchen cabinet unless she takes something out. In the past, I would have really beaten up on myself. I didn't do that and was able to take responsibility for my actions and move on.

There will always be different perspectives in a relationship. The opportunity is to allow Love to show us how to be respectful and honest with one another. In the past, my ego would have wanted me to judge and blame Pat rather than take responsibility for myself. Love is showing us a different way.

I am learning little by little that if I can live in the moment, be grateful, and trust the energy of Love, situations can be resolved in a way that doesn't require us to get upset, stressed out, and life is so much more enjoyable.

I'm really happy that after all these years, I am beginning to remember that I always have a choice in difficult situations; to get frustrated, angry, and stressed, or to stay in gratitude and in the present moment. I'm trusting there is peaceful Love energy available that offers me a solution to all of my problems if I'm open to it.

JOURNAL

Do I give my partner the freedom to do what they want?

Am I able to be honest about our differences?

Do I share what is bothering me rather than holding it in?

Chapter 27

Living in the Moment

"When you make friends with the present moment, you feel at home no matter where you are. When you don't feel at home in the NOW, no matter where you go, you will carry unease with you."
~ Eckhart Tolle

Pat:

I believe that living in the present moment is key to my peace of mind and spiritual health. Sometimes my mind is like a blender, jumping into the past or into the future. I'm in trouble when I'm in the "What ifs".

What if: I run out of money; I don't have enough energy to do what I want to do; I don't meet my soulmate; I don't get clients; my health declines; I don't have a place to live; I make a mistake; I lose my job; my business fails or my marriage fails? The list goes on and on. What are the "what ifs" in your life?

The key for me is to become *aware* when I'm *not* living in the present moment. I may notice tension in my body, irritability, or fear. I lose my peace when I try to control an outcome or a person, place, or thing.

It has been difficult for me to live in the present moment when one door is closed, and I am waiting for the next door to open. I find myself in the hallway with ego rearing its ugly head trying to pull me into the past or the future. It's easy to lose my peace when I'm in the "hallway" and don't know how things are going to work out, whether that be in business, health, finances, or relationships. It's in these "hallway" experiences (and I have had a lot of them) that my faith muscles grow stronger and I learn to trust God.

I am given the opportunity to trust and surrender to "what is". I can *choose* to complain, bang on the door, cry, or plead, or I can *choose* to wait patiently for the next door to open for guidance on what to do next. I can *choose* to trust God's perfect timing. It is always my *choice* to choose Love or fear.

I've had some health challenges (opportunities) for the past couple of months that have been scary, confusing, and frustrating. Sometimes, it feels like I'm going down a rabbit's hole trying to figure out what's wrong and what to do next. I read one book and it says to do this to heal my body and another book says to do the direct opposite. I will continue to pursue my healing, knowing Spirit is guiding me. Who do I choose to listen to, Love or fear?

- I'm listening to my body and what it needs and doesn't need.
- I'm allowing myself to feel all of my feelings including frustration, anger, fear, disappointment, and sadness.
- I'm *choosing Love*.
- I'm staying positive and grateful for what I have and not what's missing.
- I'm trusting Spirit to show me the next right step. I know that *everything* has a purpose and is for my highest good.
- I'm practicing living in the moment because the moment is all there is.
- I'm trusting my intuition.
- I'm praying, meditating, being patient, letting go and surrendering.

Instead of all the "what ifs" which is often motivated by fear about the past or future, I am living in the present moment and "acting as if". Acting as if means that if I want something, I must act as if I already have it in order to get it.

If I want to be healthy, I must act as if I am already healthy. If I want new friends, I must act as if I already have friends. If I want more money, I must act as if I have money, rather than come from a place of lack. The key is a willingness to look *beyond* my current reality, knowing that it can and will change.

I am healthy and whole, I am guided, I am protected, I am loved. My affirmation is: "Everything is flowing with peace, ease, and grace, and I have all the energy to accomplish what I want to do."

Living in the Moment

Larry:

Eckhart Tolle, in *The Power of Now* suggests that an enlightened way to live our lives is to live in the present moment, not the past or the future.

I have been attempting to adopt this philosophy in my life, with various amounts of success. When I'm able to live in the moment, I'm not stressed or worried about the past or the future. There is an energy and power that makes each moment okay. I don't have to feel afraid, stressed out, alone, or less than. All I have to do is to be open and allow myself to be loved at that moment.

For example, last Friday I received a certified letter from a US Department of Labor lawyer. The letter had a lot of complicated lawyer talk that quite frankly, I didn't understand. It was about a pension I receive, and it had the word "terminate" in it. There was a contact number, but their offices were closed until Monday.

This experience was a perfect opportunity to practice living in the moment. I had a choice; to spend the weekend worrying about the future and the possibility of losing my pension or living in the moment. Losing my pension would have significantly changed my retirement situation.

In the past, receiving a letter of this magnitude and not being able to clarify it immediately would have stressed me out, and I would have worried about it all weekend. Instead, I chose to trust the energy and light of Love.

Ego tried very hard to get me to focus on the possibility of losing my pension. I was surprised how easy it was to live in the moment once I decided to enjoy my weekend. As a matter of fact, I almost forget to call on Monday morning since I wasn't focusing on it.

I was quite surprised on Monday morning when I called the lawyer and she answered the phone. She explained in great detail that the company which I have my pension with had moved to Malaysia and the labor department was assigning a new managing company. She reassured me that I would not be losing my pension.

I could have spent the whole weekend worrying and stressing out about something that wasn't even going to happen. Instead, because of what I'm learning and practicing, I had a wonderful opportunity to live in the moment and let go of stress, worry, and the future.

One of the areas in my life that I am beginning to address is my patience level or perhaps I should say my "impatience" level. I struggle with impatience all the time. I am learning a wonderful way to address it. Eckhart Tolle suggests that when we become impatient it's because we don't want to be where we are. We want to be somewhere else doing something different or what we consider the next best thing.

The secret to dealing with my impatience is for me to live in the moment and to live in the *now*. I have been practicing this for a few months and I'm beginning to have some incredible moments when I do this. This practice has had a profound effect on my impatience. Whenever I find I'm becoming impatient (like at red lights or in lines at stores or waiting for someone), I just remind myself to be aware of the very moment I am experiencing. I bring my attention to the fact that I have absolutely everything I need in the present moment and have no reason to become impatient or need to be somewhere else.

The other day I went to the state tax department to pay my taxes. They had two windows open with about a dozen people in the line. The line was moving very slowly, and I could feel the tension growing as people were becoming impatient. One person was having a difficult time understanding what the clerk was trying to explain to her and was becoming very frustrated and anxious. I chose to stay in the present moment in peace and clarity and not allow myself to get caught up in the negative energy. I had the presence of mind to ask Love energy to be present in the environment, which helped prevent things from escalating.

I figured something out about traffic lights. There are "red light days and green light days." When I'm having a red light day, I get almost all the red traffic lights. There was a time when I would become impatient about all the red lights, but now I know I consider the red lights as opportunities to stay in the moment and send Love energy to those around me. I realize that I also have green light days when I get mostly all green lights and those give me opportunities to just keep cruising along.

Our faith and trust enable us to believe and expect that whatever happens, we will be sustained at that moment.

I missed incredible opportunities that were actually gifts along the journey when I worked long and hard to reach my goals and not live in the present moment. We make the best decisions we can at the time, according to where our consciousness is. Now I am learning to find value in the journey by living in the moment. It was fear and worry that kept me from living in the moment and the *now*. This is different from keeping my eye on the goal and what I want to accomplish in my life.

When I lived my life in fear and worry, I felt a sense of control (which is an illusion) because I thought that the fearful thoughts were real. This created constant negative energy and tension that supported my lack of trust. Although I was on a faith journey, my faith didn't provide me with the tools I needed to live in the moment.

As I am practicing living in the moment, I don't have a sense of control as I thought I had before. The more I live in the moment, the more peaceful and relaxed I feel. That is what letting go is all about for me because I am learning to trust. The more I allow myself to seek awareness and consciousness, the more confidence I have in my ability to trust in the energy and light of Love.

In retrospect and looking back over my life's journey, I always had a sense that there was *more* and that I could have it all. Today, years later in my faith journey, I have it all. If I had not traveled the journey I did, I would not be where I am today and have the consciousness that I have.

JOURNAL

Am I able to live in the moment or do I live in the past or future?

Am I able to look beyond my current situation and "act as if?"

Am I impatient and don't want to be where I'm at?

Chapter 28

Respect

"I speak to everyone in the same way, whether he is the garbage man or the president of the university."
~ *Albert Einstein*

Larry:

I recently asked myself, "Can I respect others if I don't respect myself?" I don't think so. I thought about the qualities I see in myself that I admire and respect. I see my compassion, kindness, honesty, trustworthiness, flexibility, generosity, and my ability to give and receive love.

There was a time in my life when I couldn't admit to myself that I had these qualities. It is probably because I couldn't express them perfectly. I had to get to a place where I understood that I didn't have to be perfect in order to admit I had these qualities. Perfectionism is something I have struggled with for most of my life.

For years, my self-confidence and self-respect came from what people said about me and was ego driven. Of course, living like that is like living on an emotional roller coaster, sometimes up, sometimes down, mostly all over the place depending on who I was spending time with.

In time, I began to realize it isn't important what people think or say about me. What is important is what I say about me and what I believe about myself.

Once I began to take responsibility for my life and actions, I was able to forgive others and myself. I realized I had some good qualities that I could claim as my own, even though I wasn't living them perfectly. Over the years, I have come to nurture and respect those qualities and when I see them in others, I know that I also have them.

I was thinking about how I have given my power and respect away in the past. One way was to allow friends or family to take advantage of me, guilt me, or manipulate me, especially in the name of love. Another way would be to allow others to talk to me disrespectfully (yelling, swearing, name-calling, bullying, silent treatment, etc.)

I have learned that I teach people how to treat me. When I don't set healthy boundaries and finally say "enough is enough" to inappropriate behaviors, I continue to allow myself to be disrespected. When I allow others to treat me this way, I am not respecting myself. It must start with me.

I know how difficult and painful it is to set boundaries. I've had to draw the line and inform those who, from my perspective, were treating me with disrespect. I've had to inform them that I would not accept that kind of behavior. Often it resulted in a lost friendship. I see that as a choice of either losing a relationship or losing myself. Really, if we lose ourselves, what do we have left to share?

It takes courage to say "enough is enough" when we feel disrespected by another's behavior and actions. As I have learned to respect myself, I expect to be treated with love and kindness, just as I choose to treat others.

Respect

Pat:

As I thought about my relationship with Larry, the word that stood out for me was how we *respect* one another. We give each other "space" to do what is right, trusting we know what we need to do for ourselves.

> "*Respect* means valuing each other's points of view even if we disagree with it. It means being open to being wrong. It means accepting people as they are. It means not dumping on someone because you're having a bad day. It means being polite and kind always because being kind to people is not negotiable. It means not dissing people because they're different from you. It means not gossiping about people or spreading lies." – Urban Dictionary

Whether it is in a partnership, marriage, friendship, or parent-child relationship, *respect* is crucial as the foundation. I may not agree with someone's actions and may even be concerned that it is not healthy for them, but I am learning to *trust* that they are doing the best they can and they will learn what they need to learn in their own time and way.

Who am I to judge another person's actions and think I know what's best for them or that I am right, and they are wrong? This is my ego thinking I know best. I remind myself that if I had the same life experiences as they had, I might be doing the same thing.

I thought I had the answers for my ex-husband for many years. If he just did it this way or better yet *my way*, he would be fine. I realize that I didn't want to look at myself and what needed changing in me, so it was easier to focus on him.

It didn't work. It never works trying to control someone, especially someone I love. That is not to say, I don't give my opinion *when asked.* I give my opinion and then let it go and let it be. I am practicing keeping my mouth shut when I want to get into someone else's business. It is not always easy, and I don't always do it right.

Instead of trying to control and give unsolicited advice, I pray for loved ones and send them love and light. This is how I keep myself peaceful, so I don't worry and obsess about them. It is like I am saying to the person, "I trust and respect you. I know you will do what is right for you. I will support you and I am here if you need me."

I remind myself to be patient and respectful; everyone is doing their best on their own journey. I can't force people to respect me, but I can refuse to tolerate disrespect.

JOURNAL

Can I respect others if I don't respect myself?

Where do I give my power away?

Am I able to see my good qualities?

Chapter 29

Senior Sexuality and Aging

*"Aging is not lost youth but a new stage
of opportunity and strength."*
~ Betty Friedan

Larry:

As we age our bodies begin to surrender to the pull of gravity. We develop wrinkles, our skin begins to sag, and parts of our bodies head "south". I mentioned to Pat the other day, "the skin on my neck under my chin reminds me of a turkey." Some folks experience hearing loss or their eyes aren't as sharp as they used to be. We develop cataracts, sore feet and muscles, rickety knees, and back problems that require prescription medications. We seem to spend more time in the doctor's office than anywhere else.

You may question how does this affect our sex life? I once heard that, "Love in my heart wasn't put there to stay, Love is not Love until you give it away." I love my wife and one of the ways I express that is by making love to her. It may be different than it used to be, we are in our senior years and there may be areas of our bodies that don't respond quite as well as they used to. That doesn't mean we have lost the ability to be sensitive, caring, and loving. A kiss, a hug, a soft touch can still ignite our passions as we have learned to discuss our challenges and commit to making things work to the best of our ability.

As we get older it's not always about passion; we discover other ways to show our love. We know how important it is to be there for each other when we are going through a stressful time or when we have sickness or injury.

I love Pat in many ways: by being patient and kind to her by treating her with respect, being present to her when she is sharing a concern or problem, telling her I love her during the day, a surprise shoulder massage, or kiss on her neck as I pass. I let her know that I am completely committed to her and our relationship, and endeavor to keep it loving, interesting, and vibrant.

I have mentioned before that I believe "Love is God". When I am loving Pat, I am the vessel, but it's really God loving her through me. It doesn't get any better than that.

Senior Sexuality and Aging

Pat:

I believe Spirt brought Larry into my life to help heal my sexuality and to show me unconditional love. I believe him when he says, "God is loving you through me." Larry encourages me to ask for what I want and say no to what is uncomfortable. It has taken me years to feel safe in my body and heal from the trauma of sexual abuse. I cried hysterically on my wedding night the first time I made love with my husband. It was downhill from there. I didn't remember the sexual abuse until many years into the marriage. Consequently, I endured sex rather than enjoy it.

My sexual relationship with Larry, because of our aging bodies and my history of sexual abuse is not conventional. It works beautifully for us as we experience deep intimacy by just holding each other and being open to the energy and light of love as it guides us to be in the present moment.

We have learned to respect and accept what no longer works. It is not a time to compare what other couples are doing. We have come to a place of peace and serenity and enjoy each other's bodies.

The other day Larry said to me, "Look at my hands they look *old.*" We both laughed knowing it was the truth. We know we are in the *winter* of our journey on earth. We live each day in gratitude and love. We are not promised tomorrow, and we don't know when our train is coming in. Larry says he wakes up each morning with a heart full of gratitude and ends the day with a heart full of gratitude. I do the same.

We celebrated our three year wedding anniversary recently. Here is the *Blessing of the Hands* that we said to each other on our wedding day.

BLESSINGS OF THE HANDS

There are hands of our best friend,
strong and full of love for you.
They are holding yours today as you promise to love
each other today, tomorrow, and forever.
These are the hands that will work alongside ours,
As we continue your future together.
These are the hands that will passionately love and cherish you
through the years and with the slightest touch
will comfort you like no other.
These are the hands that will hold you when
you fear or grief fills your mind.
These are the hands that will give you strength
when you need it, support, and encouragement to
pursue your dreams, and comfort you in difficult times.
Most importantly, always remember that these are God's hands
loving you. And lastly, these are the hands that even when
wrinkled and aged, will still be reaching for yours, still giving you
the same unspoken tenderness and love with just a touch.

The truth is our bodies are aging and doing what they need to do. We are invited to love our bodies as they change and to *accept* "what is" and appreciate what we do have. Rather than focusing on what's not working or missing, we focus on what is working. Let us accept and love our bodies and minds; wrinkles, crinkles, sagging, and everything else. Let us celebrate who we are and how far we have come.

One of the challenges we face as we age is the opportunity to show our love and patience by taking care of each other when we are compromised or become ill, which will eventually happen for all of us. We are also aware that one of us will be left alone when our partner transitions.

My prayer is that we will continue to welcome the aging process gracefully and allow Love's light and energy to show us the way and give us what we need.

JOURNAL

Do I accept the aging process with compassion and peace?

Do I love and accept my body as it ages?

Has sex become more or less important as I age?

What are the ways I express my love to my partner?

Chapter 30

Time

"Take the time to enjoy the dance of life while the song is still playing."
~ Linda Andrade Wheeler

Larry:

I can hardly believe that I have been retired for over nineteen years. I thought that when I retired time would slow down and I'd appreciate it more. Maybe, I was half right. I do appreciate it more, but it certainly hasn't slowed down. Retirement has given me the time to grow and become more conscious of who I am and who I want to be. Here are some of the things I've discovered:

I don't want to feel responsible for another person's
well-being or happiness.

Pat and I have a beautiful loving relationship and we understand that we are not responsible for making each other happy and providing for each other. We recognize that we are both adults who love one another and will always support each other. We treat each other as individuals and as equals. There is no pressure on either of us to provide happiness for the other, as happiness comes from within.

In the past, I have felt unworthy of the gift of Love's
energy and light.

I have learned that Love is freely given and has nothing to do with being worthy or good enough. We are magnates for Love, which is a gift that is always waiting for us to receive it. I've opened my heart to Love and I've never been happier in my life.

I'm learning what I want and what I don't want.

In the past, I didn't value myself and often did what another person wanted me to do. It was easier to not rock the boat than to express my needs or sometimes it really didn't matter. What I thought was really important was that I spent time with the person. Now, I value myself more and allow myself to make decisions depending on what I want or don't want to do, even though it may disappoint others.

I'm learning to eliminate stress from my life.

I know what causes stress in my life and, for the most part, I don't allow stressful situations to materialize. I endeavor to live one day at a time and practice living in the moment. I live a stress free life and believe it is why I'm happy and at peace with myself.

Many people are so busy every day that they don't have the *time* to do everything they would like. The days just don't seem long enough. I had a demanding career working long hours and had to take care of my family. At the end of the day, I was tired, frazzled, and exhausted. All I wanted to do was crawl into bed and collapse. I was up again the next morning doing it all again. Do you ever feel like you are on a treadmill going around and around?

Our physical and psychological bodies are incredible, but they do have a limit. When we pay attention to our bodies, they will tell us when they are reaching their limit. If we don't take the *time* to listen, they will eventually break down.

I had my own catering business for sixteen years. I remember what happened to me around Christmas. It was our busiest time of the year and my partner, Bob, and I had been going for days without stopping. I looked at him and said, "I can't do this anymore. I have to leave for a while." I felt like everything was closing in on me and I was suffocating.

I've always felt a connection to forests and wilderness. I headed for a beautiful forest and reservoir that I used to frequent when I had more *time*. I walked up a trail and into the forest. There were no other people around and it was snowing lightly. The deeper I walked into the forest, the more I began to feel the incredibly powerful energy. I felt like I wanted to hug a couple of trees. I sat down against one of them and just let the connection happen. The stress started to drain away as the snow fell gently on and around me. I don't remember how long I stayed there but when I left, I felt refreshed, renewed, and loved.

I was incredibly happy that I had listened to my body and took the *time* I needed to refresh myself. It seems to me that sometimes our priorities are out of whack and we continue to place ourselves on the bottom of the list. At the end of the day, we have no *time* left to love ourselves. When we plan on taking a trip, we know enough to fill the tank of our vehicle with gas. If we expect ourselves to address all the issues in our day, we better take the *time* to fill ourselves with the energy we will need to take us through the day.

I believe that the energy and light of Love is in every one of us. How wonderful it would be if we all started our day by taking the *time* to love ourselves first. Growing up, I was taught to be considerate of others and that it was selfish to always think about what I needed or wanted. That is true, however, that doesn't mean forgetting about myself and placing myself at the bottom of the list.

It's taken me fifty years to realize that I'm important enough to be placed on the top of my priority list. As a gift, I offer you this practice. Each morning when you wake up look into the mirror and tell yourself, "I Love You; I'm so happy that you are me and I can't wait to spend the day with you." This was difficult for me to do at first because it felt strange and unnatural. I now find it a terrific way to start my day because it fills my tank.

Time

Pat:

I struggled with being a rush-aholic and busy-aholic for many years to avoid the hole in my soul that I tried to fill with people and outside things. Busyness distracted me from my feelings and what was inside of me. I looked good on the outside, but inside I felt inadequate and didn't feel good enough, no matter what or how much I achieved.

Rushing was my addiction and had become a way of life for me. It gave me energy when I rushed. I felt powerful when I multitasked and felt in control. I used rushing and busyness to medicate painful feelings from my childhood. I always pushed myself to do more and more and didn't know how to relax or *be*. Rushing puts you into adrenaline overload and drenches the body in epinephrine, a hormone stimulated by stress, anger, or fear.

Although on the outside, I may have looked peaceful, there was an "inner rusher" that was pervasive and intense. I walked fast, I ate fast, and I drove fast. I had to get things done quickly and never took my time with anything. I felt impatient with others when they did things slower than I did.

I have learned that I disconnect from myself and from the divine energy of Love within when I rush to avoid my feelings. I'm not respecting myself or the God within.

Unfortunately, in our goal oriented society, it's about work, achieving, and getting things done. Workaholism is insidious and rampant in our world. There is a sense of control and accomplishment which makes us feel valued when we unconsciously stay busy or work to avoid feelings. Are you substituting work or staying busy because you don't want to feel your feelings? Being so busy, we tell ourselves there isn't enough time for pleasure and fun. No wonder so many people have heart disease and are stressed out.

Here is an affirmation I use, especially when I think I have too much to do and so little time to do it. "I have more than enough time to do all that is mine to do." I practice this affirmation so I don't get caught up in the old beliefs that busyness and being productive is good and relaxing and enjoying is bad. The ego tries to make me feel guilty and convince me that taking time to relax, do nothing, and enjoying the moment is wasting time.

Years ago, I couldn't relax until everyone in my family was settled and happy. I realize now that I had it backward. I know that if I don't love and nurture myself first, I cannot love and give to others.

Here are some examples of old beliefs: There's never enough time to do all that I want to do. Time is flying by. The older you get; the faster time goes. I often hear people say, "How did I ever work, I am so busy now?"

We are all given the same amount of "sacred" time each day to do what we want to do and what is important to us. Every moment, every breath is precious, and I don't take it for granted because it is a gift from God. I am not promised my next breath, and neither are you. It is my desire to live my life to the fullest and to live in joy and peace.

I ask myself before an activity, "Will this bring me joy?" At this time in my life, for the most part, I do what I want to do. I no longer push myself to try to please everyone else. If I don't know what I want to do at the moment, I ask Spirit for guidance and then just do the next right thing, which may be eating breakfast or calling one of my children. As I endeavor to live in the moment, I know that I am guided with each decision I make. It always works and I get to where I want to be.

Being retired and living on Maui with all the wonderful activities to pursue gives me the opportunity to practice *taking* the time to do what I want to do. Instead of always *doing*, I'm learning to *be*. I have learned to say no and not pressure or push myself to do everything to please others.

It's easy to get out of balance when I'm stressed. I have the tendency to push myself by staying busy, rushing, and doing too much. I know it almost immediately because I lose my peace and feel irritable. Because I want to use my *time* consciously and to enjoy the life God has given me, I practice living in the moment. I know what my priorities are and what makes me peaceful, happy, and joyful.

- Spending *time* in prayer and meditation every day.
- Loving myself and taking *time* to nurture my body, mind, and spirit.
- Spending *time* with my husband and nurturing our relationship.
- Spending quality *time* with friends and family.
- Spending *time* writing as my sacred service and being creative.
- Spending *time* doing what I love, walking in nature, dancing, playing, having fun.

I encourage you to *take the time* to enjoy your life and have fun. This is your *life*, not a dress rehearsal. Ask yourself, "What steps can I take to nurture my body, mind, and spirit today?"

> *May the God of the present moment be with me, slowing me down, revealing to me the sacred gift hidden in each moment of my day.*

JOURNAL

Do I feel responsible for my partner's well-being and happiness?

How can I eliminate stress in my life?

Do I take the time to do what I want and enjoy?

Chapter 31

Trust

"When you learn to trust yourself, you will know how to live."
~ Eleanor Roosevelt

Larry:

I think *trust* is one of the most important qualities when it comes to a committed love relationship. How do we build trust in a relationship? Just like most of us, I have been disappointed and hurt in the past by people I loved and trusted. This has happened to me more times than I would have liked.

Consequently, I have some "trust issues". It's not difficult to trust people on small things; like believing them when they tell me they are going to meet me at a certain time, or they share something that happened that day. It's easy to believe that they are sharing their perspective, and I trust it is their truth.

I asked myself, "How do I open up again to trust another person when I've been hurt, and relationships have ended?" I can trust because I value a love relationship more than my fear of getting hurt. I am willing to take full responsibility for my choices. After I have taken the time to heal and forgive, I am open to another relationship. I'm trusting this one will be successful, and to the extent that it is, we will stay together.

How do I know another person is trustworthy? Before I ask that question, I need to ask myself, "Am I trustworthy?" I think I'm trustworthy because I endeavor to be honest with myself and my partner. I look for these qualities in a relationship whether it be in a friendship or a love relationship. I'm growing and becoming more conscious daily and take full responsibility for my actions. I'm becoming more aware when the ego is influencing my life negatively and take steps to prevent that from happening.

How have I built trust in my relationship with Pat? I think honesty and respect are two qualities that have helped me to do that. I support and encourage her to be her own person and to do what's important to her, even though it may not seem important to me. Likewise, she supports and encourages me to be my own person.

Just trusting there is someone watching your back that loves you is huge, especially when you're going through a difficult time. I am confident that Pat will have my back. I've learned to trust that she will be honest with me even if she disagrees with my perspective or direction. Because of our past experiences, I know she will not agree just because it will make me feel good and, that builds trust. She also knows that I will be there for her, no matter what.

Even though we may feel hurt or disappointed in a relationship, I'm learning that being able to *trust* someone in my life is a wonderful asset. I don't have to face difficult times alone because there is someone I can confide in and will help me relieve my stress and angst. I think it's worth the risk to feel loved, supported, and protected.

I asked Pat this question: "How do we maintain our relationship with ourselves when we are in a love relationship with another person?" For many years, I ignored my relationship with myself and gave it all to the person I was in a relationship with. When the relation-ship was over, I didn't have anything to support me and felt empty.

A healthy relationship will allow each person to have a life apart from the other, friends, interests, hobbies, etc. When we have developed a relationship with ourselves, we will most likely want to spend some time alone. It isn't that we don't love the other person or don't want to be with them. I walk three miles every day and I value that time alone. When I'm driving my car, I don't use the radio because I value the time alone with myself and I enjoy my own company. If the relationship is secure and there is trust, each person would encourage and support the other in the personal relationship they have with themselves.

My experience with failed relationships has taught me that it requires a lot of work, especially on my part. I am continuously finding opportunities to change, grow, and learn and not to *resist what is*.

Sometimes I wonder why so many people are looking for that "perfect relationship"?

Sometimes we think that we will be sent that perfect person and like magic, we will live happily ever after. From my experience, that just doesn't happen. I believe a relationship is a tool to help us find out many things about ourselves. I think that's why relationships are so difficult. When there are bumps in the road, do we always blame our partner, or do we look at our response to the situation? What are some of the options available to us when we find ourselves in a challenging situation?

- We can argue and get upset.
- We can yell and scream hoping that we will get our way.
- We can calmly try to explain our perspective of the situation.
- We can recognize that the energy is not conducive to discussing the problem right now and exit the room.
- We can take time to calm down and get our emotions under control.
- We can go within to discover why the situation is so important and we may find out that it's not all that important.

Perhaps it's time to realize that loving one another reminds us that we are all connected. The one common thread that connects us is the energy and light of Love. Yes, we are all different in some ways and sometimes we say and do things that hurt each other. We are not perfect. I don't believe perfection is what it's all about.

Love will show us how to forgive, heal, and move on. I believe life's purpose is to learn how to love ourselves so we can become vessels of Love. I invite you on this journey and together we can over-come our differences and walk this journey of Love together.

Trust

Pat:

It has taken me many years of hard work to trust myself and release old beliefs and behaviors that no longer served me. I try to live in the moment and let go of the past and future. It's not always easy, but I strive for it.

Of course, while I was raising a family and holding a full-time job, I had to do things I didn't want to do, whether it was convenient or not. I didn't have a choice when I had to nurse a baby in the middle of the night or get up with a sick child. I loved being a mother and don't regret a minute of all that I did.

I didn't know then what I know now about the importance of loving and appreciating myself, self-care, and taking sacred time for myself. I had it backward. I had to take care of everyone else first (including my ex-husband and children who were old enough to take care of themselves) before I did anything for myself. I said yes when I meant no and then felt resentful when I was exhausted. I'm grateful for all I have learned and continue to learn.

Being in a relationship and married now, I know it isn't all about me and what I need and want. Larry and I work beautifully together to make our relationship harmonious. We listen to each other and nego-tiate our needs for the good of the relationship. We rarely question what the other is doing or not doing. We may suggest something to the other and then let it go if the other isn't interested. Instead of being codependent or dependent, we are interdependent.

It's interesting what happened this week when Larry was triggered by something I said. I went into the TV room and said, "I love how we respect one another's decisions to do whatever we want to do for ourselves. I feel the freedom to do what I need to do for myself and think you do too."

The Universe definitely set this up for us to communicate with one another. He looked at me and said, "I would appreciate it if you didn't question me about when I have my breakfast." I had no idea what he was talking about and asked him to explain.

Larry works on the computer in the morning and usually eats his breakfast at about eleven am. That morning he came into the kitchen at nine am and said, "I'm hungry and going to have my breakfast now."

I was surprised and innocently said, "It's only nine am; you don't ever have your breakfast at nine am." I had no intention of telling him what to do or what not to do. It was just a comment.

Larry said, "I felt judged, and like I was doing something wrong when you made that comment." We both realized he was being triggered by an old belief that no longer served him. His old belief was that he couldn't relax until he was productive and finished his work.

I could certainly relate to that belief in my own life. If I didn't check off things on my to-do list, I felt guilty that I didn't do enough. It was hard to relax and do nothing if I wasn't productive first.

We were both grateful that we recognized this old belief that keeps us from doing what we want when we want to do it. Communication, respect, trust, honesty, and vulnerability with one another are key components of a healthy relationship.

JOURNAL

What are my trust issues in our relationship?

Can I open my heart when I have been hurt in past relationships?

Do I trust myself?

Chapter 32

Truth

"If you are always trying to be normal,
you will never know how amazing you can be."
~ Maya Angelou

Pat:

As I know and embrace this truth that I am Love, the more I will see the Love in others and help them to embrace it in themselves. Remember, what we see in others, both the light and the dark is in us. You wouldn't be able to see it if it wasn't in you. I wonder why it is easier to see the darkness or shadow rather than the light in ourselves. I was told I was conceited as a young girl, and I have had to work hard to let go of that belief that doesn't serve me. It is not easy for me to affirm "I am amazing" but I practice it because I believe it is the truth and what Spirit wants all of us to do.

I am "awakening" to the truth of who *I am; I am* Love and the presence of God/Divine/Source/Essence in the world. I am a Divine being that comes from Love and is made of Love. Do you know that you are Love and the presence of God in the world or do you think you are unworthy, not perfect, or not good enough to even consider that?

Do you see how amazing and loving you are, or do you only see where you need to grow and change? Ask Spirit to help you *remember* who you are. You are *Love*, here to love and be loved.

"When you affirm 'I am amazing' to yourself, you are not only affirming it for yourself but for everyone else because we are all *one* and connected."

I see it in you and invite you to see it in yourself. *You are amazing* and the presence of the Divine in the world.

The Greatest Love Story is You

You are a Divine Spiritual Being and you are here to bring light and love to the world. This is what you have been waiting for as the world needs your light. Love is your purpose and mission on earth.

> *Say yes to be the light and love that I call you to be today. The world is awakening to the truth that we are all one and not separate from God. You know the truth and will share it with those I send to you. Do not be afraid of your light for it is my light shining through you. There is much darkness in the world that is now coming into the light. Although it looks like things in the world are deteriorating and people are very anxious and confused, it is my plan being played out. There is no need to be afraid because this has been planned by me and is the beginning of a great awakening.*

We believe that *Love is all there is.* It is all around us, within and without, and available to us right now. Each person has within them their own great Love story. Whether single or married, rich or poor, when you look at life through loving eyes, you are happy and have the only real wealth there is Love—and the awareness of the light shining within your soul.

Say *yes* to the greatest love story ever told. *You* are the light shining in the darkness and everything you need is inside of you.

JOURNAL

Do I believe I am amazing?

Do I know that I am Love?

Is it easier to see my shadow than it is to see my light?

Chapter 33

Amazing Spiritual Experience

"Death is nothing more than a doorway, something you walk through."
~ George Ritchie

Larry:

I would like to share an incredible experience I had one morning three years ago, although there are no words to adequately describe what happened.

As I lay on my bed, my form dissolved and I became one with Spirit. I immediately became one with the universe, one with God.

As I experienced being released from form, I felt free and light, as though an anchor was removed from me. There was an energy that I had never experienced before that some would describe as a near-death experience.

I was thrilled and ecstatic, I felt like I had arrived home. I had no fear and felt extreme, unconditional love, value, and acceptance. I was *one* with God and all creation.

For me, this incredible experience was a beautiful confirmation that:

- Love is all there is.
- God is the energy and light of Love.
- All creation is connected as cells in the body of Love.

When we transition, we are not ending our journey we are just approaching the starting line, we will return home to the most incredible existence you can imagine.

I share this profound experience with you because it has had an incredible effect on my life and perspective of Love. It showed me that

Love is all there is. I now have no fear of transitioning from form to Spirit.

Anita Moorjani shares in her book *Dying to Be Me*, from the other side,

> *"I became aware that we're all connected . . . . Everything belongs to an infinite Whole. I was intricately, inseparably enmeshed with all of life. We're all facets of that unity—we're all One, and each of us has an effect on the collective Whole."*

For some reason, I had been given a preview or taste of what is to come after our journey in form. I did not have to earn or become worthy to receive this gift. I received it because I am part of the whole of creation, (just like you are.) We are all connected through Love; we are one with all.

JOURNAL

What has been my most amazing spiritual experience?

Have I ever had that experience of being one with God or the Universe?

Do I fear transitioning from form to Spirit?

Conclusion

We want to thank you for reading *It's Never Too Late for Love*. It is our hope that we have inspired you in some way and given you hope that the desires of your heart will be fulfilled, if you are patient and trust God's perfect plan and timing for your life.

We've attempted to share with you our experience of choosing the element of "Love Consciousness" in our relationship. We hope you find your path to "Love Consciousness" whether you are single, married, in a relationship, or looking for one. As long as your heart is beating, "Love" is waiting for you to accept the free gift that Love is. The world looks like it's going down the tubes. Eckhart Tolle teaches, "The world is getting better and worse at the same time, you always hear about the negative because it makes more noise." Millions of people all over the world are choosing "Love Consciousness". Be good to yourself, choose "Love".

The message I received ten years ago from God has manifested and I am living my dream.

> *"You must wait and then you will be ready. I will surprise you with a Love that is far more wonderful than you could ever dream of."*

To those yet looking for soul mate Love, know that it can happen if you are patient and trust God's perfect timing. To those questioning your partnership, you will be reminded that Love is a choice you make every day. It takes patience, respect, honesty, and understanding to grow and evolve. To those of you already living a life in Love, you will be given another reason to celebrate life's journey.

God's divine timing is perfect. It is never late and always on time. Love found later in life can have a depth and maturity that is uncommon in younger years. It is worth the wait to be patient and trust. The best is yet to come!

The path to manifesting your heart's desire and living in Love.

- *Choose Love*
- *Face your fears*
- *Live in Faith*
- *Follow your Heart*
- *Accept "What is"*
- *Forgive*
- *Practice Gratitude*
- *Trust*
- *Let go and Let God*

God is faithful to His word. We continue to grow and evolve each day as a couple. We encourage you to open your heart to the energy and light of Love and experience heaven on earth.

Acknowledgments

We are deeply thankful to Sharon Lund for transforming our manuscript into this book and bringing it out into the world.

Thank you, Kaitie Palm, for editing our book and your encouragement.

We extend our heart filled gratitude to John Laney for his early review of the manuscript and his helpful feedback.

We are thankful to Kat Place for reviewing our manuscript and writing the foreword for our book.

We are grateful to Robert Place for the photo cover of our book.

We thank Nancy Harris and Donna Rustigian Mac for their support and feedback while writing our manuscript.

We sincerely want to thank everyone who believed in our love story and endorsed our book.

We would like to thank each other for making this difficult work a very pleasant experience, by being open, flexible, and leaving our egos at home. We are grateful to the energy and light of Love for being our strength while leading us to the completion of this book.

Meet the Authors

Pat and Larry Burns

Pat Burns is the author of the book, *Simply a Woman of Faith* in which she shares her personal stories of faith and love. Pat has been on her spiritual journey for over forty-five years. She obtained her bachelor's degree from Roger Williams University in Bristol, Rhode Island, and her master's degree from Springfield College in New Hampshire. She was a Licensed Alcohol and Drug Therapist, as well as an International Retreat and Workshop Leader for twenty years before retiring to Maui in 2011. Pat is presently a Spiritual Life Coach helping women learn how to love themselves, find love, and manifest their heart's desire.

Larry Burns has been called by his friends, "Mr. Love". Larry has been on his spiritual path for over fifty years. This journey led him to involvement in non-violent protests against war and nuclear weapons in the seventies and eighties. He was involved in feeding the homeless and deprived in the community. Larry owned a successful catering business and managed a large industrial cafeteria for thirty years. He was retired for six years before moving to Maui in 2007.

Pat and Larry love to laugh, write, have fun, and relax. They enjoy dancing together and their life on Maui, where they continue to evolve and grow on their spiritual journey.

To contact Pat or Larry, please visit their website:
www.It'sNeverTooLateforLoveBook.com